TURN BACK YOUR
FACE YEARS

A Personalized Handbook For Beautiful Skin

BY RICHARD ASARCH, M.D.
WITH MARIA WEST

Ideal Publishing
Denver, CO

Turn Back Your Face Years: A Personalized Handbook for Beautiful Skin by Richard Asarch, M.D. and Maria West—2nd ed.

1. Health – Miscellanea. 2. Beauty – Miscellanea.
3. Medical – Miscellanea.

SECOND EDITION
ISBN 0-9724665-1-7

Second Printing, August 2003

TO MY WIFE, ELAINE,

Your vision, support and encouragement have always been the foundation of my accomplishments.

ACKNOWLEDGEMENTS

The impetus for this book originated from a very special group of people, my patients. Over the years, I have appreciated their trust and their queries regarding their skin care, allowing me to seek answers and solutions to their problems and concerns. My teachers and mentors in the field of dermatology and lasers are too numerous to mention. I am deeply grateful to everyone who has played an important role in the understanding and development of my skin care programs and procedures.

Special thank yous go to Allen Fahden, who encouraged me to complete this project, and who added his wit and wisdom. To Pat Wanderer, for proofing and editing the text. To Maria West, for her countless hours with the composition, preparation and organization of the manuscript. To my children Deborah and David Landy, Jodi and Chad Asarch, Jonathan, Adam and David Asarch, for inspiring me. And to my parents, for their confidence and support for as long as I can remember.

TABLE OF CONTENTS

Introduction

EVERYWHERE YOU GO, YOUR FACE GETS THERE FIRST

Over a decade ago a mini-skirt-clad Gloria Steinem, looking lively and sensual, strode onto the stage of the Jay Leno show. Leno was in shock. "You look great," he told her. "Aren't you 50?

"This is what 50 looks like," she smiled.

What does it mean when someone looks good for their age? What does 40 look like? Fifty? Sixty? Our lives are getting longer, but we still look older, dismissed by a youth-centered society?

How do you stay healthy and vibrant? Why do some people look 20 years younger than others the same age? Genes, exercise, style, nutrition and happiness play a part. But we have all seen a 50-year-old in excellent athletic shape, but marked with wrinkled, leathery skin that makes her look two decades older.

Your skin health is a connected reflection of your aliveness and vibrancy. You can color your hair, work out regularly, dress expertly and carry yourself with poise, but your skin can still be a mask of damage and lines that hides your true self from others. As we age, many of us discover that the face in the mirror no longer looks like the self we know.

Nationally, we spend billions of dollars on skin care. Cosmetic and supplement companies offer incredible numbers of products. Doctors keep adopting more and more sophisticated methods to remove wrinkles and create younger-looking skin. Many pricey lotions and creams promise incredible science-based miracles, but contain useless fillers. People will spend any amount necessary for smooth, youthful looking skin. The question is: What works?

Thousands of theories about skin bombard you from television, magazines and cosmetic-counter attendants. What will really help your skin, and what is merely snake oil that will leave you poorer and with the same or more damaged skin than you had before?

Of all the treatments, what should you use and at what stage of your life? How can you sort through the hype to find the right skin care for you?

You need trained scientists and dermatologists to point to products and procedures scientifically proven in controlled studies. Over 25 years of practicing medicine, I have adopted the latest advances in cosmetic dermatology as soon as science proves that they work.

I began using lasers for skin conditions two decades ago. I constantly search for the easiest, most effective treatments for my patients. I seek out the latest findings and most recently available procedures, products and research. I will show you how to create and maintain glowing, healthy skin.

Many of the books on skin care are so thick and intricately detailed that it is difficult to discover and sort out what will help you personally. Another problem is that, ironically, just reading about healthy practices or exercise can actually make you feel as if you have done them. But reading or skimming a book rarely translates into concrete lifestyle changes.

Face Years was designed for you to use every day with your skin care routine, as well as when you make major decisions on procedures for your skin.

We overview the secrets to beautiful skin but also pinpoint your specific needs. You can tear out the removable charts, personalized to you. Hang the regimen chart by your bathroom mirror, and take the ingredient chart to the cosmetics counter.

Face Years is a simple, easy-to-use guide for keeping your skin healthy and young looking. First, you will find out what skin type you have. Then you will learn the stages of aging and the most current procedures for the challenges of each stage.

Next, you will discover the right program for your skin, with cleansing, moisturizing, nutrition and treatments for your specific issues. We will sort through the myths and hype about skin, arming you with everything you need to have the healthiest, most youthful skin possible, using up-to-date research and medical technology.

Finally, you have a personalized handbook for healthy, beautiful skin. It will allow you to diagnose the current condition of your skin and find out what you can do to have the skin you want. Then you can tear out the chart summarizing the procedures and product ingredients that will help you.

How Old Are You in Face years?
And How Do You Turn Back the Clock?
Most people who want healthier skin ask two basic questions:

1. Can I get noticeable results without huge expenses or invasive procedures?

2. How can I make sense out of all the claims made by skin-care companies?

Both questions make the same point:
What really works and how do I use it?

Chapter 1

HOW OLD ARE YOU IN FACE YEARS?

When we are born our skin fits like an elastic, resilient glove protecting our bodies. When we change from plump babies with rolls and ringlets, to taller, active, thinner children, our skin contracts, leaving only as much as we need to cover our bodies.

As we age and spend time outside exposed to ultraviolet light, our skin changes. We develop small imperfections in skin color, tone and elasticity. Eventually, unwanted bumps, growths and wrinkles appear.

Most people do not know exactly when these nuisances appeared but see them slowly becoming apparent. Over time, these changes reveal our Face Years.

Depending on heredity, skin color, environment and ultraviolet light exposure, your actual age may be different from the age your skin suggests to others or what you see when you look in the mirror.

Now you can evaluate your skin and find out how old it is in Face Years. You will group the changes associated with aging into six characteristics: Lines or wrinkles, pigment changes, skin-color changes, textural changes, blood vessels and precancerous changes. I will have you rate how severe each condition is. Your score will tell you how old you are in Face Years.

Look at the following pages for the chart. Familiarize yourself with the different characteristics.

Next, sit in front of a mirror in a well-lit room. Relax all of your facial muscles, no smiles and no squinting. If you need to, wear your glasses, but it would be easier to use a magnified mirror.

Using the scoring scale from 0 (absent) to 3 (very pronounced), circle the number which most closely fits your facial skin. When you have completed all of the columns, simply total all of the numbers you circled. Take this number and go to the results table to see how old you are in Face Years

The Face Years Test

DIRECTIONS: **Circle the number that rates your skin on each of these conditions.**

Lines: Expression lines or wrinkles present at rest, accentuated during expression.

Pigment Changes: Discoloration of the skin, mostly brownish flat areas.

Skin Color Changes: Yellowish cast to the skin.

Textural Changes: Irregular, bumpy surface on skin.

Blood Vessels: Tiny blood vessels are visible on skin.

Precancerous: Dry, red, scaly precancerous lesions present.

EVALUATION SCALE	
SCORE	PREVELANCE
0	Absent
1/2	Very early changes or visibility
1	Visible but mild
2	More pronounced
3	Very pronounced

Use the above Evaluation Scale as a guide to circle your answers on the next page and, then see the results that follow.

FACE YEARS TEST					
LINES	PIGMENT CHANGES CHANGES	SKIN COLOR	TEXTURE CHANGES	BLOOD VESSELS	PRECANCEROUS
0	0	0	0	0	0
1/2	1/2	1/2	1/2	1/2	1/2
1	1	1	1	1	1
2	2	2	2	2	2
3	3	3	3	3	3

RESULTS	
TOTAL SCORE	AGE IN FACE YEARS
0	20 – 25
1/2 – 3	26 – 34
3 1/2 – 6	35 – 49
6 1/2 – 6	50 – 64
12 1/2 – 18	65 – 75

Now that you know how old your skin is in Face Years, read Chapter 2 on what causes aging skin. Then use Chapter 3 on page 19 to find out what products and procedures will help your specific situation. Chapter 3 has a section for each Face Years stage.

Chapter 2

HOW YOUR SKIN AGES, HEALS, CONCEALS AND REVEALS

There are almost as many myths about how your skin works as there are products to exploit the myths. To successfully navigate the hype of sales clerks and the lure of magic potions, you need to understand how your skin ages, heals and protects you.

The skin is your body's largest organ. In an average person, stretched out, it would cover 20 square feet, the equivalent of a cover for a very small Honda. Three layers make up your skin:

1. The outer protective layer (epidermis), about 0.1mm thick.

2. The middle layer (dermis), which can vary from 1mm to 4mm in thickness.

3. The fat layer (subcutaneous), which varies dramatically in people depending on their body types and weight.

Your First Line of Defense: The Epidermis

The extremely thin protective layer called the epidermis contains several layers of cells. The cells resemble a brick wall, with new cells produced at the base of the layer.

As new cells form, older ones migrate toward the surface, losing moisture and flattening out as they go. By the time they reach the surface, the cells have died. They slowly slough off as new cells move up.

The epidermis serves as a protective barrier, preserving moisture and preventing irritating materials and germs from entering the body.

The Meat of Your Skin: The Dermis

The dermis layer accounts for almost 90% of the skin's mass and contains many major parts of the skin: connective tissue, small blood vessels, sweat glands, oil glands, nerves, and cells that produce collagen, called fibroblasts.

Two important fibers named collagen and elastin weave throughout the dermis, giving skin flexibility, tone, durability and firmness.

The Fatty Layer of Your Skin

This subcutaneous layer is composed of loose connective tissue and fat tissue that varies with your body fat. This layer cushions the skin and contributes to skin contours. It also insulates and stores energy.

Aging

The signs we associate most with aging are the visible changes we see in our skin, especially on our faces.

Though your body ages in many ways, wrinkling and lessened elasticity in your skin make you look older. By minimizing the signs of aging in your skin, you change how others perceive you.

As Time Goes By, Your Skin's Elasticity Goes With It

Skin ages in two ways: Ultraviolet light damage and natural breakdown over time. Chronological or intrinsic aging is simply a matter of what happens to our skin over time without any external causes. Obviously, this happens to everyone's skin, whether sun-exposed or not.

The Sun Ages You Faster Than the Years

We call the damage done to our skin by the sun and other sources of ultraviolet light, photoaging. Wrinkles, dehydration and abnormal skin cells result from sun exposure more than from skin breaking down over time.

Our susceptibility varies with the ability of our skin to produce pigment which will protect against ultraviolet light. You will read more about this in Chapter 4.

Hormones

For women, estrogen plays a significant role in the firmness, flexibility, moisture and even the color and texture of skin.

When your estrogen levels decline, the dermis loses collagen and elastin. The skin becomes drier and less flexible. Estrogen deficiency speeds up your skin's aging.

That Saggy Look

With aging the epidermis becomes more permeable and more susceptible to irritation from the outside. The skin cells that make up the epidermis start to break up and lose their neat, brick-wall-like alignment.

Skin makes fewer new epidermal cells, and so the epidermis becomes thinner. The pigment cells located in the bottom layer of the epidermis decrease in number, but the remaining ones get bigger. Oil and hair production also go down. The result: Aging skin appears thinner, paler and blotchy.

In the dermis, collagen fibers diminish. These fibers have more cross links, which make them stiffer and less resistant to pulling. With time, these cross links decrease and skin tears more easily.

The elastic fibers get thicker and stiffer and become clumped together. They lose their ability to recoil, giving skin a loose, hanging appearance. Blood vessels become more fragile, which can lead to bruising. Sweat glands can also decrease, and the sebaceous glands produce less oil.

The connective tissue loosens in the fatty subcutaneous layer, and skin starts to sag.

Skin Heals More Slowly as You Age

When you severely injure your skin, the wound disrupts the skin's integrity. Healing means the structure and function become restored. In most cases, the skin spontaneously closes over the wound in the next several days, protecting the structures underneath by restoring continuity. This happens as cells with different structures in the skin follow a set pattern of multiplying and filling in the wound. Skin cells migrate from the edges to bridge the gap and allow more advanced healing.

If you have a wound, keep it moist by covering it with white petrolatum or an antibiotic ointment. It will heal in a shorter time than if it is dry and crusted.

Ultimately, wounds transform into mostly collagen fibers, or scar tissue. Fiber bundles enlarge and produce a dense collagen structure, the scar. All scars slowly change in bulk and form over the years.

Unfortunately, aging skin repairs itself more slowly than younger skin, taking wounds up to four times longer to heal. Older patients produce fewer cells, and these cells have shorter life spans. Poor circulation and skin nutrition make the problem even worse.

As you choose products and procedures to rejuvenate your skin, keep in mind that collagen, elastin, circulation and nutrition all play major roles in aging skin. These are the best places to start the healing.

The 3 Basic Skin Types

There are 3 basic types: normal, dry and oily. Another factor you must consider in your skin care is whether your skin has areas of increased hyperpigmentation. Heredity often determines what skin type you have. Your correct nutritional and reparative regimen depends on your skin type and whether or not you have increased pigmentation. Different regimens can be found in Chapter 10.

People with normal skin have few problems with most skin care products. Their skin can withstand frequent cleansing, application of astringents, moisturizers and make-up without developing problems.

Dry or sensitive skin allows small cracks or fissures to appear in the skin's outer layer, resulting in a barrier loss. Irritants can lead to inflammation, redness and discomfort. Skin care should restore the correct moisture level in the skin and avoid irritation. Sun exposure and dry climates will aggravate dry/sensitive skin.

Oily skin requires products that will remove the excess oil for varying amounts of time. Some newer products contain small microspheres that can absorb excess oil. Traveling to a hot and humid climate will make oily skin worse.

For hyperpigmentation in any skin type, you need to apply sunscreen frequently. Bleaching products can gradually lighten the skin. Remember, with ultraviolet light exposure, hyperpigmented skin will produced pigment much faster than lightening creams can lighten it. Stay out of the sun!

Chapter 3

"DID SHE?" LOSE YOUR FACE YEARS, KEEP YOUR MYSTERY

What Is Aging?

Some celebrity magazines have made a minor religion out of celebrating women who continue to look young and lovely into their 30s, 40s, 50s and beyond. In most of the photographs, these women have no imperfections or lines of any kind.

Movie stars and singers often tout eating right and staying happy as their beauty secrets. Rarely will one admit to using special skin products, let alone having major or minor procedures to keep skin smooth, plump and glowing. But these celebrities are often the best customers of cosmetic surgeons and dermatologists.

No matter how well you eat or take care of yourself, your body will age as your skin thins and wrinkles. Your face will droop, and small blood vessels and age spots will appear. Few of us have purified, sun-filtered lifestyles, so we have more signs of aging or even skin cancer.

Once you have damage, how can you turn back the clock on your Face Years?

What to Expect With Each Face Years Stage

20 - 25
IN FACE YEARS

You have minimal changes, so take preventive measures to keep your skin healthy.

Treatments for This Stage:
Sunscreens
Moisturizers

A preventive program of:
Tretinoin (Renova or Retin-A) or Tazarotene(Tazorac)
Topical antioxidants
Collagen-stimulating agents.

You can have macro or microdermabrasion or light peels. Use Botox in areas with accentuated furrows (between eyebrows, on forehead, or on crow's feet). Over time these repeated expressions lead to permanent wrinkles.

26 - 34
IN FACE YEARS

Early fine wrinkling
Few pigment age brown spots
Rare precancerous lesions
Minimal blood vessels on face
Requires little or no make-up

Fine lines at rest, minimal discoloration, perhaps a few blood vessels and textural changes.

Treatments for This Stage:
Sunscreens
Moisturizers

A preventative program of:
Tretinoin (Renova or Retin-A) or Tazarotene (Tazorac)
Topical antioxidants
Collagen stimulating agents

You should have a regular program of macro or microdermabrasion, light chemical peels, non-ablative lasers and Botox for furrows. Also consider collagen or filling material injections.

35 - 49
IN FACE YEARS

Early wrinkling smile lines
Slight yellowing of skin
Mild pigment changes, including
Brown age spots
Mild blood vessels on face

Early reddish precancerous lesions
Make-up often required

Wrinkles at rest are more apparent, as are more pronounced skin changes, splotchier skin tone, textural thickening, blood vessels, perhaps precancerous lesions.

Treatments for This Stage:
Sunscreens
Moisturizers
Tretinoin (Renova or Retin-A) or Tazarotene) (Tazorac)
Topical antioxidants
Collagen-stimulating agents
Regular program of macro or microdermabrasion
Light chemical peels
Non-ablative lasers
Pulsed-light treatments
Radio Frequency for Skin Tightening
Botox for furrows (also in neck)
Collagen or filling-material injections

In addition to the above, deeper chemical peels (tricholoroacetic acid); laser resurfacing mostly around mouth and eyes; non-ablative lasers. Laser blepharoplasty for droopy eyelids or under-eye bags.

50 - 64
IN FACE YEARS
Moderate wrinkling when skin is at rest
Obvious yellowing skin
Some pigment change, like brown age spots
Moderate blood vessels on face
Thick, scabby precancerous lesions
Need make-up to even skin color and tone

Deeper wrinkles at rest, progression of above changes. More likely to have more precancerous lesions, even early skin cancers.

Treatments for This Stage:
Sunscreens
Moisturizers
Tretinoin (Renova or Retin-A) or Tazarotene (Tazorac)
Topical antioxidants
Collagen-stimulating agents
Regular program macro or microdermabrasion
Light chemical peels

Deeper chemical peels
Non-ablative laser rejuvenation
Pulsed-light treatments
Radio Frequency for Skin Tightening
Botox for furrows
Collagen or filling-material injections

In addition to the above, laser rejuvenation for full face. Laser blepharoplasty for droopy eyelids or fat protrusion of lower lids. Botox in areas also for bands in neck. Treatment of precancerous lesions by doctor.

65 - 75 IN FACE YEARS
Severe wrinkling at rest
Loose, lax skin from sun, gravity and expressions
Yellowish cast to skin
Significant pigment changes
Moderate blood vessels on face
Precancerous and skin cancers
Need heavy make-up

Treatments for This Stage:
Sunscreens
Moisturizers
Tretinoin (Renova or Retin-A) or Tazarotene (Tazorac)
Topical antioxidants
Collagen-stimulating agents
Regular program macro or microdermabrasion
Light chemical peels
Non-ablative lasers
Pulsed-light treatments
Radio Frequency for Skin Tightening
Botox for furrows and in bands in neck
Collagen or filling-material injections
Laser rejuvenation for full face
Laser blepharoplasty eyelids and under-eye bags

These treatments improve your skin's appearance but may not tighten it enough. To get rid of unwanted sagging skin, consider a surgical face lift or brow lift.

Lose Your Face Years, Keep Your Mystery
Turn Your Face Back Decades

PROBLEM	SOLUTION
Sagging, droopy eyelids Bags under the eyes	Laser blepharoplasty
Facial lines and sun damage	Laser rejuvenation Chemical peel (medium)
Mild to moderate sagging skin	Radio-Frequency and neck skin tightening
Deep depressions on face (Such as smile lines framing your mouth)	Collagen Permanent implants Filling substances

Droopy Eyelids, Under-Eye Bags
Blepharoplasty with a Laser Heals Much Faster

Many patients complain that their eyes are framed in wrinkles, droop, or have bags of bulging skin under them that make them look tired and years older. Droopy eyelids and bags under the eyes are some of the easiest signs of aging to correct.

Laser blepharoplasty surgery can correct all of these eye problems. You can have it done at the same time as other facial surgical procedures, such as laser skin resurfacing, to minimize healing downtime.

Unlike regular blepharoplasty using a scalpel, it takes only days for laser blepharoplasty to heal. You can easily have it done on a Friday, take a week's vacation from work (or just a couple of days if you have only the lower lids done) and return to co-workers' comments on how rested and radiant you look.

What are the advantages of using a laser instead of eye surgery done with knives? One of the potential complications of regular blepharoplasty is bleeding. But with laser blepharoplasty, the laser seals the small blood vessels and greatly minimizes the possibility of bleeding. This allows the doctor to see the area better during the procedure. More importantly, you heal days and even weeks faster, with much less bruising than if you had gone under the knife.

Questions and Answers About Laser Blepharoplasty

1. Are there stitches or sutures? After your doctor removes the excess skin of the upper eyelids, he or she sutures the skin edges together. The sutures will come out in seven days. For Laser blepharoplasty on the lower lids, you won't need sutures.

2. How long does the procedure take? That depends on whether you treat the upper eyelids, the lower eyelids or both the upper and lower eyelids. Usually, it lasts from one to one and a half hours.

3. Am I asleep during the procedure? No, but often an anesthesiologist will give you medication through an IV. This conscious sedation allows you to relax and avoid discomfort.

4. What do I have to do after the procedure? You will use antibiotic ointment or drops to lubricate your skin and prevent infection. Ice compresses during the first 24 hours help reduce swelling.

5. When can I return to work? If you have only the lower eyelids done, you can usually return to work in 48 hours. With the upper eyelids, you will have some slight bruising but can return to work without looking excessively swollen in less than a week.

Eyelid surgery makes patients look dramatically younger and more alive. A beautiful woman in her late 40s named Jo came to me concerned that her eyes made her look tired and worn out all of the time. After the surgery, she told me that people keep commenting on how big her eyes look. The procedure gave her confidence when working with clients. "The other day I ran into someone I hadn't seen in a while," she reported. "He said, 'Don't you get any older?' I loved it! That's exactly the result I wanted."

Facial Lines and Sun Damage
Laser Skin Resurfacing: The Liftless Facelift

A few years ago laser skin resurfacing became popular until rumors started that it was a traumatic procedure whose benefits had been exaggerated. But laser surgery breakthroughs in the last few years have made laser skin resurfacing a safer, easier way to eliminate wrinkles than traditional face-lifts or plastic surgery.

Patients looking for dramatic, permanent changes in their skin often choose resurfacing. They come away amazed at their dewy, new-looking skin. Though the first week takes a full-time commitment to recovery, you can completely return to your normal routine in seven to ten days.

Laser skin resurfacing removes surface imperfections while smoothing lines and wrinkles without an invasive face-lift. Carbon dioxide lasers create the most dramatic changes. For technical reasons, I recommend the UltraPulse5000c Aesthetic Laser. For a slightly lighter procedure, the Erbium 2.94 Laser lets your doctor remove layers of skin less than a thousandth of an inch thick.

The laser peels off years of sun-damaged skin. It removes wrinkled skin layer by layer, stimulating the regeneration of the deeper healthier skin. The laser's powerfully focused beams of light create heat that destroys cells. Unlike dermabrasion and chemical peels, lasers use high-energy beams of light to vaporize scars, lines, wrinkles and other skin defects.

Precise, controlled lasers used by a trained physician make the procedure safe and predictable. The laser instantly vaporizes only the outer layer of skin, minimizing the risk of injuring the surrounding tissue with scarring or pigmentation changes.

The Benefits of Laser Resurfacing
Laser skin resurfacing's two major effects are:

1. Removing damaged cells and
2. Tightening the underlying collagen.

Its cosmetic benefits include:

- It noticeably reduces deeply-wrinkled skin beneath eyes without invasive, scalpel procedures

- It smoothes crow's feet around eyes

- It vaporizes high ridges of wrinkles

- It makes skin much smoother

- It diminishes and often removes the lines around the mouth that cause lipstick to "bleed"

- It erases acne scars better than anything else

- It stimulates the deeper layers of skin, making it healthier and younger looking

- It gets rid of unwanted skin conditions instantly.

The earliest carbon dioxide lasers removed warts and unwanted growths, but they could damage and scar skin around the treated area. This limited their uses.

Doctors still use the old lasers to remove skin lesions, but now pinpoint precision laser technology in area and depth allows physicians to paint away lines, wrinkles, sun-damaged or aging skin.

Doctors can perform laser resurfacing in their offices with a local anesthetic and without the risk of patient hospitalization. When having a large area treated, many patients choose conscious sedation by an anesthesiologist.

Laser resurfacing involves much less pain and healing time than a face-lift. With the carbon dioxide laser you will not bleed. However, you will need to take a week off from your normal routine.

After the surgery, you will wear a face bandage the first day. Some physicians just use the bandages, but keeping the skin underneath moist with wet compresses reduces discomfort, and makes you heal faster with less risk of infection.

When your doctor takes the bandage off, your skin will scab unless you constantly rinse it with saline (salt) solution. You must continue this time-consuming process for six days. The saline rinse speeds the healing time by several weeks and creates smoother, more beautiful skin. When you sleep or move around, cover your skin with petroleum jelly to keep it moist. You don't want your skin to dry out. Your doctor should give you day-to-day instructions.

Because laser surgery requires no invasive cutting, your skin should heal in seven to ten days. The more you soak with saline, the faster and more smoothly it will heal. Stock up on saline beforehand.

For the next several weeks, your skin will vary from red to pink. This results from the production of new blood vessels under the skin, which promote healing. Once the skin has healed, the vessels gradually disappear and the redness fades. You can use make-up once the top layer of skin has healed, which is usually in seven to ten days.

Ecstatic patients report that friends and acquaintances who know nothing of their treatment tell them they look ten to twenty years younger. Keith, a 57-year-old man whose athletic past in the outdoors had left him with wrinkled, scaly skin and quite a few precancerous lesions asked me how he could best help his skin. "In the seventies all I did in my spare time was play tennis and hang out on the beach. Now my skin makes me look like an old man," he said. Concerned about his cancer risks, Keith was excited to hear about all the things laser resurfacing could do for him.

"I dedicated myself to sitting in the bathtub and rinsing my face with saline for the first week afterwards," Keith reported on his laser resurfacing. "My wife thought I looked scary, but it didn't feel that bad."

Laser resurfacing made Keith look like a new man. "Everyone thinks I'm in my forties," he told me. "Just last week I met a guy who said he was happy to meet someone else in his mid-forties. He couldn't believe that I'm almost 57. In business it really helps to not look like I'm over the hill. It's so great to like the way I look again. Erasing all of those precancerous spots is just a miracle."

Radio-Frequency Skin Tightening
The Surgery Free Facelift

Now doctors can use radio frequency to stimulate collagen deep within your skin without affecting the outer layer. This activates aging collagen, bringing firmness and youth to your skin without any healing time. This decreases wrinkles and tightens loose facial skin without any time away from work or anyone knowing you had a procedure at all.

The new radio frequency device, the ThermaCool TC System, delivers higher energies to a larger area than non-ablative lasers. In a few seconds the ThermaCool system delivers treatment to selected areas of skin in three steps. First, a cooling spray allows heat to safely travel past the top layers of skin to reach collagen in the deeper layer. Next the skin is treated with heating, then finally by a post-treatment cooling. Your doctor controls the depth and area he or she treats.

Scientific studies prove that radio frequency tightens and increases collagen in deeper skin layers without damaging the outside skin. Clinical studies also show that this results in less wrinkles and tighter skin.

The major advantage to radio frequency is that there is no healing or down time. You can exercise, go to work, wear make-up, and continue your daily life uninterrupted. How much skin tightens varies with the patient. You can repeat the procedure for greater results. It takes 3-4 months to see the full improvement one radio frequency treatment will make to your skin.

Fillers for Deep Depressions (Smile Lines)

Many of my patients complain about deep lines or depressions where the cheeks meet the upper lip in the bottom half of their faces. As cheek skin sags, it rests against skin around the mouth, producing a deep wrinkle that makes you look years older.

Doctors use fillers like as bovine collagen, your own fat. human engineered collagen, or bio-polymer hybrids to soften this and other deep lines. American doctors have successfully used purified collagen to fill deep lines for years. Doctors in Europe and Canada can use fillers like hyaluronic acid gel, and micronized plastic spheres/bovine collagen, but as of the writing of this book, the FDA has not approved these for the United States.

Recently the FDA has approved human-engineered collagen made from human cell cultures. With human collagen you don't need the allergy skin test you did with bovine collagen, and the filled-in look lasts longer.

The doctor places collagen at the base of the groove to fill or soften it. This new collagen breaks down slowly, so you need injections every three to six months.

A doctor can also place a permanent Gortex implant shaped like a pliable hollow tube in the depression. The doctor makes two tiny incisions: one by the nose and one near the corner of the mouth. He then threads the tube under the skin and leaves it there. Your skin gradually produces a fibrous material that grows into the tube and incorporates it into the dermal layer of your skin. The tube can be removed if it causes problems or if you don't like the results. Occasionally you can see the tube when you make extreme expressions. A newer basket-weave implant has been developed to minimize this problem.

Chemical Peels

The major difference between chemical peels is the depth that they penetrate the skin.

Linda, 47, had spent plenty of time in the sun in her youth. She wanted a deep, dramatic change in her skin. "My skin was really blotchy because I used to worship the sun," she reported. "The medium chemical peel felt like a bad sunburn. It took ten days to heal." She was ecstatic with the results. "It took away all the brown spots, and got rid of my crow's feet. It made my face pristine. It was hard to go through the healing, but it was really worth it."

Consult the chart on the following page to understand the differences between superficial chemical peels and deeper peels.

CHEMICAL PEELS				
DEPTH	AGENT USED	PENETRATION	IT HELPS	HEALING TIME
Superficial Peels	Alpha Hydroxy Acid:	Though still superficial, peel depth in top of the epidermis varies by Glycolic Acid concentration.	Superficial changes Discoloration Fine Lines	Usually redness for an hour Sometimes mild crusting for 3-5 days.
	Beta Hydroxy Acid Salicylic Acid	Same as above.	Same as above.	Same as above.
	Trichloroacetic Acid 15% - 25%	Just a little deeper than above.	Same as above; also neck & chest. Helps discoloration.	Scaling or crusting for 5-7 days.
Medium Peel	Trichloroacetic Acid 35%	The depth goes to the upper dermis.	Fine to medium facial lines. Actinic Keratoses	Significant crusting 7-8 days. Skin will stay pink for 3+ weeks.
Deep Peel	Phenol Peel	Deep to the reticular dermis.	As above but deeper lines. Risk heart side effects & scarring. Risk loss of pigment.	Crusting & blistering which resolves in 2+ weeks. Several weeks to heal.

Turn Your Face Back Years

PROBLEM	SOLUTION
Facial lines on forehead between eyebrows and outside eyes	Botox injections
Facial lines	Non-ablative lasers or Macro or microdermabrasion Pulsed-light treatments Radio-frequency skin tightening
Depressions or scars	Collagen or filler injections
Skin texture changes	Salt peels
Fine lines	Macro or microdermabrasion
Facial blood vessels or brown spots	Lasers Pulsed-light treatments
Spider veins	Sclerotherapy
Excess hair	Laser hair removal Pulsed-light treatments

Botox Injections
Facial Lines from Repeated Expressions

Deep facial lines begin as temporary creases where muscles make favorite expressions over and over. Over time, the underlying collagen develops a memory of this crease. Your skin's loss of elasticity prevents it from returning to its smooth resting position.

Botox can prevent these unwanted lines as well as smooth the ones you already have.

The common places that develop expression lines:

AREA	MUSCLES INVOLVED
Between eyebrows	Corrugator superciliaris muscles draw the medial ends of the brow.
Eyebrows frown	Procerus muscle pulls the skin, causing horizontal creases at the root of the nose.

Area	Muscles Involved
Crow's feet on outside corners of eyes	Orbicularis oculi muscles
Forehead	Frontalis muscle

Facts About Botox

1. Botox is a potent neurotoxin produced by the bacterium Clostridium Botulinum.

2. The toxin inhibits the release of acetyl choline at nerve endings, paralyzing the treated facial muscles. This prevents you from making the unwanted expression.

3. You usually notice results in two to six days. The effects slowly wear off over three to six months.

4. The dose and the location of injections may vary slightly from person to person.

5. Botox injections pose no permanent risks. However, sometimes additional muscles in the vicinity of injections may accidentally relax, too. This wears off quickly since very little Botox reaches these muscles.

    a. Eyelids can get droopy if Botox reaches the tiny muscle that lifts the eyelid. If this happens remember that it will not affect your eye. The "lazy" eyelid usually returns to normal in a few days but might last a few weeks. Your doctor can often counter act the problem by prescribing Iopidine 0.5% ophthalmic drops, which you apply to the affected eye three to four times a day.

    b. If too much Botox acts on the lower part of the forehead muscle, your brow can droop. Wait a few weeks for it to wear off, or contact your doctor. Sometimes your doctor can inject small amounts of Botox around the brow to minimize this until the Botox gradually wears off.

6. If you take the following medications, notify your physician before having Botox injected: Aminoglycosides, penicillamine, quinine and calcium channel blockers. They can affect the amount of Botox required.

Botox can make a noticeable difference in your appearance at any age. Sherry, a woman in her late 20s had vigilantly stayed out of the sun since she was 16. She had the smooth skin of a twenty-year-old, except on her forehead. At 26 this animated woman had started to see permanent creases in her forehead from raising her eyebrows, and lines between her eyes from furrowing her brows.

"For a year, I tried not furrowing my brow to keep the lines from getting deeper. I didn't have crow's feet like a lot of my friends who used to lay in the sun, but my forehead made me look older than I was."

She was excited to hear about Botox injections, though the idea of putting a toxin in her skin worried her. After talking with older friends who raved about it, she finally took the plunge. "I'm so happy!" she told me. "I can't make those expressions anymore, but I don't even notice it. I feel like I'm still frowning, but I'm not. The best part was that the wrinkles that I thought were permanent have completely gone away. The only downside is having to come in every three to six months to get it redone. But it's worth it. Those lines were becoming tread marks on my forehead."

Lasers That Stimulate Collagen

Lasers can now stimulate collagen in the dermal layer of the skin without injuring the top layer. If you have avoided laser rejuvenation because of the healing time involved, or if you need a touch up but want a no effort post-treatment course, non-ablative lasers can do it. They can reduce wrinkles and turn back time on your collagen clock.

These lasers can reduce wrinkles on all skin types with the following advantages:

- Painless
- No postoperative wound care
- No post-treatment evidence of procedure
- Non-invasive and do not need local or general anesthesia
- Allow you to return to normal life right away
- Can be done in the office.

Basically there are two different types of non-ablative lasers that differ in the wavelengths they use. The shorter-wavelength pulse-dye lasers interact with the small vessels in the upper dermis. They irritate the vessels, stimulating collagen production. At too high an energy level they can cause mild, temporary bruising, so look for an experienced laser surgeon.

The other laser uses a longer wavelength, which acts deeper in the dermis and not on blood vessels. It also stimulates the production of new collagen. There is no risk of bruising with this type of laser.

Non-ablative wrinkle reduction requires multiple treatments. Usually 4 treatments at 4-6 week intervals work best. Maintenance treatments at 3-4 month intervals help maintain the improvement. Benefits can range from less than 10% reduction in wrinkles to more than 50%. Most people have a 25-30% reduction of their lines and wrinkles. Combining both types of non-ablative lasers may improve the results.

Ruth, a longtime patient of mine, complained to me about the wrinkles around her mouth. "My mouth has the worst wrinkles," she pointed out. "They make me look like an old lady. I don't want to get a face-lift. Everyone I know who has one ends up looking really extreme and strange. It's really obvious that they had surgery. Besides, the whole idea of having my skin peeled back is really disgusting. My friends have told me how much it hurts." Ruth had a series of non-ablative laser treatments just around her mouth. Her painless monthly treatments lasted for less than five minutes each over five months. "About halfway through I thought it wasn't working at all, but I kept up with it," she told me. "By the fourth month I could see a big difference. And even after the treatments it keeps getting better. I guess that's the collagen stimulation. I like what I see in the mirror so much more now. My daughter lives out of state, and every time she visits she tells me that my skin looks even better than the last time. And you know how critical children can be. That tells me that it's made a huge difference."

Facial Blood Vessels
Many people think "broken" blood vessels on the nose and cheeks are a sign of alcoholism. In reality, facial blood vessels

usually become dilated or slightly larger from sun damage, though alcohol abuse and a rich diet can make them worse.

Different lasers or intense pulsed-light sources can clear up visible blood vessels. An experienced dermatologist can treat them quickly in the office with no down time. The laser will "erase" the vessels with no crusting or bruising.

You will probably have a pinkness for an hour to an hour and a half, but you can put on make-up right away. You may need two to three treatment sessions, depending on how many blood vessels you have. The Nd:YAG laser works best for superficial blood vessels.

How Lasers and Pulsed Intense Light Remove Facial Blood Vessels

1. The laser or pulsed light passes through the top layers of skin without affecting them.

2. Once it passes through the skin, it reaches the underlying blood vessels. The color of the blood in the vessel attracts the laser or pulsed light and absorbs its energy, creating heat and sealing the vessels.

3. Immediately after the treatment, your skin will look pink or red. When the redness subsides (usually in 30 - 60 minutes), you might see small blood vessels in the skin. These are remnants of the sealed vessels. Allow four weeks for them to absorb. Wait four to six weeks between treatments to see if you need another one.

4. Some vessels may reopen later and require another session. You will see improvement every time, but it varies from patient to patient.

5. Once the vessels disappear completely, they will not come back. However, since sun exposure by age 18 usually causes them, new vessels can appear later.

6. Often a temporary redness is the only sign of laser or pulsed light sealing. Some people develop a small crusting after treating a large vessel, but can still put on make-up right away. It will disappear in a day or two.

The Nd:YAG laser effectively treats individual blood vessels that you can see on your skin, even ones you can see only when you stretch your skin. However, if your skin has a pink or red flushed appearance but no distinct vessels, a pulsed-dye laser or pulsed intense light may be better. Redness means you have a network of vessels deep under the skin. Since you can't pick out individual vessels, the laser or light source focuses on a spot seven to ten millimeters in diameter. The pulsed dye laser may make the vessels explode, creating bruises which can last for 10 to 14 days. If you do get a bruise, you might find it hard to hide with make-up. It will go away. Over-the-counter DermaBlend make-up can cover it. Mineral powder make-up for post-op laser resurfacing patients also works.

Make sure you use sunscreen afterwards. If you expose unprotected skin to the sun, it becomes red as the blood vessels in the skin get bigger. This can open up the vessels you sealed, reversing the procedure.

Treating facial blood vessels is fast and easy. "I used to feel so self conscious about these red blood vessels on the tip of my nose," 25-year-old Jon told me. "I couldn't believe that they were gone in just two doctor visits. It was just like -- zap! And they were gone. I wished I'd known about it earlier."

Brown Age Spots
You can have age spots anywhere on your body, but may notice them more on your face, hands and arms. While a skin laser can take care of these, intense pulsed-light treatments also work well, and are faster and less costly. The treated areas become dry and scaly, then peel away in five to seven days. You may need two to four treatments depending on how dark your spots are. There are rarely complications with age-spot removal.

Beverly, a 56 year old woman who looked ten years younger than her age, was so excited to hear she could remove her age spots. "I was always trying to hide this brown spot on my forehead with make-up. I couldn't do much about the age spots on my hands. I thought they were inevitable. After the treatment, they dried up and just fell off in a few days. Now I don't have those 'age' signs anymore. I'm a grandmother, but I don't want to look like one."

Smooth Skin with Salt Peels

Salt Peels have become important for treating aging, sun-damaged skin, pigmentation marks and even fine lines or wrinkles. It provides a gentle, effective, mechanical peeling of the skin called macrodermabrasion, using salt crystals to remove dead skin cells. You can have it along with your regular skin health program.

Its origin relates to an earlier discovery. In the mid-1980s Italian doctors introduced microdermabrasion using aluminum oxide crystals. Major advantages include:

1. The procedure is painless
2. You won't need anesthesia
3. You may repeat treatments as often as you wish
4. Treatments do not interfere with normal life.

Microdermabrasion uses a vacuum to draw the aluminum crystals to the skin surface and to take them away. This can injure and bruise very sensitive skin.

The newer macrodermabrasion sprays salt crystals with a positive pressure over the skin. The focused, powerful stream of fine crystals leaves skin smooth and fresh. You can also have macro-dermabrasion on your neck, hands or chest. Using ultrasound after a salt peel can help topical nutrients to deeply penetrate skin, increasing their effectiveness. The entire treatment usually takes about an hour.

Patients find these peels as relaxing as a facial massage. You can usually put on make-up within an hour. You will see more immediate results with salt peels than with superficial or glycolic chemical peels.

Initially start with a series of six peels, then regular maintenance every three months to enhance the effects. Your skin texture will improve, any irregular pigmentation will fade and your fine lines will diminish.

Integrating macrodermabrasion with a daily routine of proven skin-repairing products, such as as tretinoin (Retin-A) or tazarotene (Tazorac) and topical antioxidants, gives excellent results. If the skin has more significant damage or changes, you might consider a medium-depth chemical peel or laser skin resurfacing.

Spider Veins

Many women have spider veins, or telangiectasias, on their legs. These small purple or red veins, sometimes called sunburst or starburst vessels, can form anywhere from the top of the thigh to the ankle.

While spider veins do not pose major health problems, many sufferers find them embarrassing and try to hide them with clothes or cosmetics.

We often inherit the tendency to develop spider veins, especially those on the upper thighs. Other causes include pregnancy and prolonged standing or sitting, both of which increase pressure in the veins of the legs. Hormones, especially estrogen, may also contribute.

A simple treatment called sclerotherapy can correct unwanted spider veins in your legs. Your doctor injects a small amount of concentrated salt solution into your vein. This displaces the blood in the vein and irritates the lining of the blood vessels. The inflamed veins swell and slowly seal themselves off. Each vein or cluster of veins may require several sessions to make them permanently disappear. You can evaluate the final response to each treatment after three to five weeks.

This extremely safe procedure has few risks. Occasionally, a small dark area of pigmentation may appear, gradually fading with time. Patients who stand or sit for long periods of time may have some swelling.

If a doctor uses too much concentrated saline, it can inflame an underlying vein. This condition, thrombophlebitis, needs immediate medical attention.

Many different lasers have also been used to treat spider veins. Sclerotherapy is faster, less painful, much less expensive and has fewer side effects or complications. Lasers will still require several treatments.

Sonja was 34, but three pregnancies had left her legs criss-crossed with spider veins. "I felt self-conscious wearing sun-dresses and swimsuits in the summer. My husband said he did-n't mind them, but they bugged me every day. It took a few sessions, but you can't see them at all anymore. I feel like I have my old body back. Now I can wear whatever I want without worrying about it."

Although no one has discovered a clear-cut way to prevent spider veins, support hose, weight control and exercise can help.

Hair Removal: A Leap Forward

Unwanted hair may not make you look older, but is still a top beauty concern. Laser and/or pulsed intense light hair removal work better than anything else I have found for getting rid of hair. These light sources are designed to effectively remove hair much faster, more reliably and more comfortably than methods like electrolysis and electrothermolysis.

The laser or light beam targets the pigment (color) located in hair follicles. It works best on light-skinned people with dark hair because of the pigment sensitivity. The laser emits its light for only a fraction of a second, just long enough to heat the pigment, destroying or impeding the hair's ability to regrow, but not long enough to affect the surrounding skin.

Most laser or light sources use a cooling tip or spray to protect the skin while directing the laser energy to the hair follicle. You recover rapidly and return to normal activities immediately. Since these light sources are attracted to pigment, it is best to avoid tanning in the areas you wish to have hair removal. If the over-lying skin is dark, the laser or pulsed light can cause blistering.

Marion, a 26-year-old patient wanted laser hair removal because her hair grew so fast and shaving left her skin irritated. "I always had bumps on my bikini line, and never had really smooth skin on my calves after shaving." Three sessions later she had much thinner hair. "I hardly have to shave my bikini line and underarms now. I never thought my calves would look this good, though I think I need one or two more treatments. It's great not to shave every day anymore."

Since laser or pulsed light hair removal usually takes several sessions with one to three months between each session, don't expect to come in one day and be ready for the beach the next. Many of my patients plan for their hair removal in the fall or winter so they can enjoy the next summer without shaving. Since you can have irritated skin for a week or so after the treatment, plan it around boating season or beach vacations.

Take Time When Changing Your Face

You can see that you have many choices when it comes to healing and preserving your skin. But don't let the sheer number of options overwhelm you. Examine the rest of the book and see how to take good care of your skin on a daily basis. First take the time to incorporate some new habits and products into your skin-care routine. Then weigh your skin procedure alternatives carefully. Most importantly, remember that you get to decide what face you'll present to the world. So go ahead and take charge of your Face Years.

Chapter 4

"TANNING" IS WHAT YOU DO TO LEATHER

What Your Mother Didn't Know or Didn't Tell You
You Age Your Own Skin Every Day

Before you turn back the clock, stop pushing it forward. Nothing will make your skin as beautiful as not destroying it in the first place.

Remember back to the old days before you knew the sun was dangerous? You would slather baby oil over your skin to tan faster. You used cardboard wrapped with aluminum foil as a reflector to trap even more of the sun's rays.

Lying in the heat of the noonday sun, you'd carefully turn to tan front and back equally. Your well intended mother urged you to "go out and get some sun" and "get some color in your cheeks." Your very health was gauged by how pale you were or if your face glowed a raspberry color.

Unfortunately, while you enjoy the warmth of the sun, it causes DNA mutations to your skin. **Your skin tans only as a means to protect itself from further injury.**

On your face, sun damage leaves deep wrinkles, freckles, brown spots, and superficial blood vessels. Your skin actually becomes thinner and loses its elasticity.

The ultraviolet rays that affect the skin are both the shorter UVB rays and the longer UVA rays. UVB are the rays that cause sunburns. Years of accumulated UVB damage can cause the skin to develop precancerous lesions and ultimately skin cancers. UVA rays cause aging by penetrating deeper into the skin, breaking down the skin's supporting structure, elastin and collagen.

Both UVA and UVB rays have been implicated in the development of melanomas. The sun also emits a very harmful third type of ray, UVC, which is filtered out by the ozone layers. As the ozone continues to thin, we may experience more effects from UVC.

You have heard the dire warnings about the sun, but even after the skin cancer hype of the last few years, many people still want a dark tan, or at least "a little color." They trade the instant gratification of today's tan for wrinkles and perhaps cancer in the future.

Remember, your skin tans only because it is injured. Think of that the next time you see a "healthy" tan. Does the skin on fried chicken look healthy?

The Secret to Gorgeous, Healthy Skin: Stop Hurting It!

Those of us over 25 have done most of the damage already. In fact, almost 80% of our total lifetime sun exposure occurs by age 18! However, we can keep it from getting worse with simple, free ways to prevent wrinkles and minimize aging.

Whatever beauty you get from lying in the sun, remember that it has a price: Aging. It can start in your early 20s and lead to wrinkled, damaged skin all over your body, getting worse as the years pass.

The Sun Causes 90% of "Aging" Skin

Even a little bit of sun hurts. Sun damage accumulates over your life. A small dose every day, every week or just every summer makes the overall damage much greater.

Some people who like to have a tan decide at a young age that they will have plastic surgery later in their lives. As a dermatologist who has treated thousands of skin cancers and performed countless cosmetic procedures, I guarantee that no matter what you do to your skin, it will be healthier and more attractive if you stay out of the sun now. Continuing to expose yourself to ultraviolet light (including tanning beds) will reverse the benefits of any cosmetic skin procedure you have done.

Sun: Bad. Sunscreen: Good

Not convinced? Well, sun exposure is also the major cause of skin cancer, a disease that has become epidemic. About a million people suffer from skin cancer each year. Melanoma, the most threatening form of skin cancer, claims almost 8,000 lives annually (American Cancer Society). Skin cancer is one of the most common forms of cancer for people in their late 20s.

All Sunscreens Are Not Created Equal

The best cure for sun damage is to prevent it. Potent sunscreens now allow you to enjoy the outdoors while protecting you from the sun.

Sunscreens use two main types of ingredients: physical and chemical blockers. The physical blockers are fine particles of metal, most often zinc or titanium, that put a thin reflective coating on the skin. The chemical blockers absorb the sun's rays.

When shopping for sunscreens look particularly at the chemical blockers. Cinnamates (octyl methoxcinnamate and cinoxate) are commonly used chemical UVB blockers added to cosmetics. You can sometimes find chemical UVA blockers called Benzophenones (oxybenzone and dioxybenzone) added to make-up. Look also for Parsol 1789, a potent UVA blocker.

Use no less than SPF 30, and make certain the label says it blocks out both UVB and UVA rays. Wear sunscreen everyday (even on cloudy days) and put it on evenly. You want to protect your skin from the sun exposure it gets even from walking out to your car.

You need at least an ounce of sunscreen to cover your whole body. With intense sun exposure, reapply sunscreen every couple of hours, especially if your skin gets wet. I realize that this sounds pretty compulsive, but the sun truly is that big a threat to your skin. The sooner you understand this, the healthier your skin will be.

Researchers are now examining how ultraviolet light affects individual skin cells. Once we understand ultraviolet light damage on a cellular level, more effective sun protection will emerge. Investigators are also experimenting with antioxidants that might stop or reduce harmful free radicals. Someday, scientists might even develop a pill to protect us from the sun.

Shield Yourself More in the Mountains

Sun damage gets worse the farther you go above sea level. A recent study revealed that exposure to UVB at high altitudes raises your risk of skin cancer, even during winter. Ultraviolet levels at 8,500 feet in Vail, Colorado, are about 40% higher than at sea level in New York City. Ultraviolet intensity increases by 5% to 8% for each 1,000-foot increase in elevation.

What About "Safe" Tanning in a Salon?

Many tanning salons claim that they give you a safe tan.

Bad news: There is no safe tanning. Indoor tanning salons predominantly use UVA radiation. Although not as potent as UVB, UVA also has both short-term and long-term effects.

The consequences of short term indoor tanning include redness, itching and dry skin. Long term you will have sagging, wrinkled skin, precancerous changes and possible skin cancers.

If You Must Have a Tan, How About a Sunless One?

Despite all of us nagging doctors, people still like a tan. If you find you just can't live with the pale look, get a safe tan in a bottle from your local pharmacy or department store.

Self-tanning products contain a chemical called dihydroxyacetone (DHA), a skin dye made from sugar. The FDA has approved it as a colorant. Manufacturers have used it safely for over 30 years. Recently, a second agent, Erythrulose, has been shown to complement DHA, producing a more even and bronze-looking tan.

While DHA and Erythrulose appear to color just the upper layer of skin, proteins in the skin actually react with it to form melanoids, colored substances that resemble melanin (the natural substance in skin that gives it its color). DHA and Erythrulose stick only to the outer layer of cells, so color fades as skin sheds.

Applying a sunless tan takes a little practice and patience. Scrub your skin lightly with a loofah or washcloth to wash away dead skin cells. Dry and then apply the self-tanning lotion in even strokes on the areas where you want some color.

Be a little more sparing on bony areas, like elbows, knees and ankles. Use the palm of your hand rather than fingertips to apply the lotion. Wash your hands thoroughly afterwards so your palms don't "tan."

Getting the color you want may take several applications. DHA products need about three hours to show the full effect of each application. Since the effects of Erythulose take to 6 to 8 hours, wait before reapplying the cream. It takes 30 minutes for the lotion to dry.

Your tan will last, but you must reapply the tanning lotion every few days. Although it may be a little time consuming, sunless tanning is the only healthful way to have that "healthy" look. And it takes much less time than lying out in the sun.

REMEMBER, even though your skin may appear "tan," the color from self-tanners does NOT protect you from sun exposure. You must use adequate sun screens with an SPF of 30 or higher. Be even more vigilant about thoroughly applying sunscreens when using a self-tanner because the darker color of your skin can keep you from seeing the warning signs of a sunburn.

The most essential beauty secret you will ever hear is to not get a suntan or sunburn.

Hurt Your Children for Life:
Let Them Play Outside Without Sunscreen

Most sun damage occurs before our 18th birthdays, the greatest in early childhood. Skin cancer frequently occurs on the sites of severe sunburns. Melanoma, the most deadly type of skin cancer, most often occurs in people who experienced painful sunburns as children.

Parents need to make sure children wear sunscreen every day, and wear t-shirts in the water at the beach or in outdoor pools. You must take care of your child's delicate skin at this pivotal time.

Painful sunburns should not be an expected part of childhood. They damage your children's skin for life. Don't ignore the danger of a sunny day.

Myths of the Sun God

MYTH: Skin cancer happens only to people with a history of severe sunburns.

FACT: While people who sunburn easily have a greater risk of developing skin cancer, sun exposure can cause cancer if you have never sunburned but had long-term sun exposure.

MYTH: Tanning is healthy.

FACT: Our skin tans, producing pigment, only as a response to injury from the sun's ultraviolet rays. After exposure, specialized cells produce melanin, a darkening pigment manufactured by our skin. Long term exposure over the years leads to brown spots, blotches, wrinkles and the appearance of small, dilated blood vessels on the skin.

MYTH: Skin will heal itself if you just stay out of the sun.

FACT: Early in life your skin can repair the trauma from ultraviolet rays, but the cumulative destruction adds up. Eventually, skin cannot repair itself, and permanent injuries and wrinkles appear.

MYTH: UVA rays from tanning booths are safe and do not harm your skin.

FACT: Exposure to both UVB and UVA radiation threatens unprotected eyes and skin. Though tanning salons may say their booths have only UVA rays, these still wreak havoc on your skin.

MYTH: The coolness in the mountains makes the sun safer there.

FACT: Just the opposite. At high altitudes the sun's intensity is much higher than at sea level. Although temperatures may be cooler, the sun injures your skin even faster higher above sea level, so you need even more protection.

MYTH: People need a great deal of natural sunlight because the skin needs the Vitamin D it manufactures when exposed to ultraviolet light.

FACT: The skin needs only a very limited amount of sun exposure to help make Vitamin D. Dairy products and many other foods are fortified and provide all the Vitamin D you need.

Always Use Protection

Follow the proceeding tips to protect your skin and still enjoy the outdoors.

1. You need to wear sunscreen every day, no matter where you live. Use one with an SPF (sun protection factor) of at least 30.

2. Apply sunscreen liberally to all exposed parts of your body and rub in well. You usually need to reapply it every two to three hours. Read the label carefully since "waterproof" may only protect you for 80 minutes. Several sunscreens on the market are waterproof for four to five hours.

3. When possible wear a hat and clothes that cover arms and legs. Materials with a tight weave provide the maximum protection. Loose-weave clothing lets sun rays reach your skin.

4. Try to avoid the sun when the rays are most intense, between 10 a.m. and 3 p.m.

5. If your shadow is shorter than you are, stay out of the sun.

6. Overcast or cloudy days do not give any protection from the sun's rays.

7. If you are taking medication, check with your doctor to see if sun exposure can cause side effects.

8. Be careful when you are around reflective surfaces like snow, water or even sand. They give you a double dose of the sun's power.

9. Avoid tanning salons. UV-light exposure that causes tanning does injure your skin. Long-term exposure increases your risk of developing skin cancer. The UVA rays in tanning beds actually penetrate and damage your skin more deeply than the sun. **Tanning salons are not safe!**

10. **Keep infants out of the sun at all times. Sunscreens should always be used on children over six months of age.**

11. Teach your children the importance of sun protection. Skin damage from the sun begins with our first exposure and continues to add up during our lifetimes.

How to Heal a Sunburn

1. Prevent the sunburn in the first place.

2. As soon as you realize you've sunburned, take two aspirin every four hours to reduce inflammation.

3. Get out of the sun right away. If you can't, cover yourself. Avoid the sun until skin heals.

4. Cool compresses soothe the discomfort. Apply them several times a day for 15-20 minutes, but no more. Longer can hurt skin.

5. Apply a sunburn moisturizing cream. You can find some designed to numb the pain.

6. If your sunburn causes extreme pain, redness or blistering, consult your doctor. You may need a prescription anesthetic lotion or antibiotics to prevent infection of the wound.

Do You Get It Yet?

So my point in this chapter is stay out of the sun! It's bad, bad, bad! While the sun is warm, inviting and fun to enjoy, it gives off harmful radiation in the form of ultraviolet rays that hurt your skin on a cellular level and ultimately can lead to dangerous cancers. Protect yourself from the sun every day.

Chapter 5

YOU WASTE HALF YOUR MONEY AT THE COSMETICS COUNTER. BUT WHICH HALF?

What to Look for in Cosmetics

Every advertisement or cosmetic sales person seems to offer a different theory on keeping skin young, healthy and beautiful.

When you walk into the cosmetic section of a department store, the colorful displays all vie for your attention. But sleek, alluring packaging doesn't mean that what is inside contains effective ingredients. You need to carefully analyze what you hear from salespeople and from the media. Read the label's ingredients. If a sales person makes a claim about anti-aging, wrinkle removal, etc, ask what ingredients make this possible.

Since I can't analyze every product available, I will identify the ingredients proven to have the most benefit on revitalizing skin.

"Dermatologist-tested" means the manufacturer sent product samples to at least one dermatologist. It does not ensure controlled studies, or even that the company followed up with doctors doing the "tests."

Calling something "anti-aging" may just mean it has sunscreen, since sun damage is the primary cause of aging skin. There are no guidelines for how much sunscreen a product must contain to call itself antiaging, so "anti-aging" doesn't mean much.

What Does Work?

Scientists have proven that certain agents do help. Don't be confused by sound-alike ingredients. Look for the following exact ingredients in your skin products. Some may be difficult to locate. Because my patients have had a hard time finding these ingredients, I created products with high concentrations of these scientifically proven agents. It's easier to design products that work than to ask people to sort through a sea of products designed for profit rather than effectiveness.

The most effective ingredients for your skin:

Tretinoin (Retin-A, Renova or Avita) (by prescription)
Tazarotene (Tazorac) (by prescription)
Alpha Hydroxy Acids
Antioxidants
Vitamin C
Vitamin E
Alpha Lipoic Acid
MDI
Glucosamine HCL
KTTKS
Niacinamide
Beta-Glucan
Retinol
Furfuryladenine
Hyaluronic Acid
CoEnzyme Q10

Retinoids (Retin-A & Tazorac): The Fountain of Youth?

Extensive research shows that topical retinoids (tretinoin and tazarotene) can reduce fine wrinkles and skin roughness, increase the thickness of the top layer of the skin and stimulate collagen deeper in the skin. All of this produces healthier, younger-looking skin. Your skin can continue to improve for up to a year of continual use. Tretinoin (Retin-A, Renova or Avita) is a form of retinoic acid related to vitamin A. All forms of tretinoin require a doctor's prescription. Tazarotene (Tazorac) is a more recently developed retinoid that has been shown to have similar effects as tretinoin. It also requires a doctor's prescription.

The retinoids' most common side effects are skin irritation and a slight increase in sun sensitivity. You can minimize this by using products with a lesser concentration of tretinoin or tazarotene.

The original Retin-A was meant to peel skin on acne patients, so it can be quite drying and irritating. Renova, another tretinoin product, has an emollient or moisturizing base, markedly reducing the dryness and irritation that occurs with Retin-A. Other products, like Avita, have smaller tretinoin concentrations, decreasing the chance of irritation.

Apply these products sparingly, and only in the evening. If they do irritate you, remember that your skin may get used to it over time.

Tretinoin can also be a very effective treatment for **stretch marks**. To reduce stretch marks, apply a tretinoin product every day for three months. If the treated area becomes too dry and itchy, discontinue it for a day or two and then use it every two or three nights. Most patients will have some improvement of their stretch marks, and many will have their stretch marks significantly reduced.

Alpha Hydroxy Acids: The Skin Miracle

Several years ago, Alpha Hydroxy Acids (AHAs) emerged as the new miracle for skin. They peel away old skin like nothing seen before.

AHAs work differently according to their concentration, so they can work for you in different types of products. After all, you don't want a daily moisturizer with the intensity of a deep chemical peel.

AHAs are a group of organic carboxylic acids used for centuries to moisturize, cleanse, improve texture and smooth skin. They originally came from natural products, like sugar cane, apples, grapes, lemons, sauerkraut and sour milk, each containing its own kind of AHA. Glycolic is the most popular. Today you can also find synthetically produced AHAs.

AHAs have been widely used the past several years. In high-strength peels (35-70%), they improve mildly-aged, sun-damaged skin. They also thicken skin and increase collagen.

Most cosmetics and moisturizers with glycolic acid have a concentration between 5% and 12%. The benefits of these over-the-counter products aren't clear. At 35% to 70% glycolic acid can penetrate more deeply into the skin and act as a superficial peeling agent.

Alpha Hydroxy Acid peels reduce scaliness and roughness, improving surface appearance. You can have acid peels weekly, bimonthly or monthly, depending on skin damage and skin sensitivity.

Scientists have not determined exactly how AHAs work. We believe they slowly dissolve the glue that holds the cells together in the top layer of the skin. This causes mild shedding, which reduces flakiness and smoothes skin.

Over time these peels may increase collagen in deeper layers of the skin. Routine AHA peels make your skin thicker, smoother, softer and less wrinkled.

Antioxidants
Free radicals which are produced by our skin during normal metabolism, smoking, sun exposure and exposure to pollutants, are a major contributor to skin aging. Topical antioxidants (vitamin C, vitamin E, and alpha lipoic acid) have been shown to inhibit the destructive properties of free radicals in the skin.

Most Vitamin C Products Waste Your Time and Money
Free radicals produced by your skin can damage the supporting structure and make you age faster. Vitamin C (ascorbic acid) is a powerful antioxidant, which means it prevents the formation of these free radicals for you.

Vitamin C also helps produce collagen, which keeps your skin firm. You need vitamin C to rebuild collagen and reduce wrinkles. However, many vitamin C creams won't t help you much. Even if they have L-ascorbic acid, the active form of vitamin C, most products can't keep the vitamin stable and absorbable by the skin Newer vitamin C lotions with ingredients such as Trisodium ascorbyl phosphate and Ascorbyl tetraisopalmitate are water-based and far more stable. This keeps the vitamin C's healing effects effective and powerful.

Many higher potency products with vitamin C also contain the amino acid tyrosine. Tyrosine may contribute to hyper-pigmented skin. Patients with hyperpigmented skin should avoid tyrosine and be careful about vitamin C products that contain it.

Vitamin E
The potent antioxidant Vitamin E protects cell membranes against free-radical damage. On animal skin, vitamin E cream reduces cell production, sunburn redness and swelling.

Alpha Lipoic Acid
Antioxidants help prevent the formation of free radicals, a major cause of aging. Alpha Lipoic Acid, a potent antioxidant, works like a normal antioxidant getting rid of free radicals. Your body routinely converts some of it into dihydrolipoic acid, an even more powerful antioxidant. Alpha Lipoic Acid is a super antioxidant. More and more products now include it.

MDI Complex
The marine enzyme MDI complex works as a 100% water soluble preservative system. It reduces collagenase, a substance in your skin that breaks down your skin's foundation of collagen.

MDI complex also keeps skin cells bonded to one another and contributes to skin's firmness and elasticity. It also retards skin sagging and fine lines, decreases skin redness and reduces the appearance of dark circles under the eyes. Now there's a cosmetic I can endorse.

Glucosamine HCL/Algae/Yeast/Urea
Testing has shown that this product improves collagen synthesis and helps skin to stay moist.

KTTKS (lysine-threonine-threonine-lysine-serine)
A pentapeptide that helps reduce wrinkles and renews the skin's outer layer by regenerating damaged skin. It also stimulates collagen production and improves skin thickness

Niacinamide
Studies have shown its ability to strengthen skin barrier integrity, reduce water-loss from the skin and increase the formation of lipid components of the skin.

Beta Glucan

Increase skin's resistance to ultraviolet radiation. It also protects against water loss.

Retinol

Although its name is similar, retinol is a different derivative of vitamin A than tretinoin (Retin-A, Renova, Avita). Limited data shows that retinol helps the skin, but not nearly as much as tretinoin. Retinol is easier to get since it doesn't require a prescription and appears in many over-the-counter products. It also rarely irritates your skin as much as tretinoin might.

Furfuryladenine

Furfuryladenine is a natural plant-growth factor that slows the aging process in plants. Leaves that have been cut will not turn brown if they are dipped in furfuryladenine. Studies indicate that furfuryladenine cream has a similar effect on human skin cells, slowing and perhaps reversing changes that occur in the aging process. Few products contain this ingredient, sometimes called kinectin.

Hyaluronic Acid

Youthful skin has lots of hyaluronic acid. A jellylike substance with a high concentration of hyaluronic acid fills the space between the columns of collagen and elastic fibers. It helps transport essential nutrients to the live cells of the skin. Free radicals break it down. It helps the skin retain moisture.

CoEnzyme Q10

CoEnzyme Q10, also known as ubiquinone, is a fat-soluble vitamin that our bodies produce to help protect cells from free radicals. Doctors recommend it to prevent heart disease. Since levels of CoEnzyme Q10 decrease as we age, some physicians feel that free radicals associated with heart problems may also cause skin aging. CoEnzyme Q10 may have the same beneficial effects on the skin that it does on the heart. Early studies are encouraging, but the jury is still out.

Like So Much Snake Oil

You now know which ingredients can help your skin, but what about the other "miracles" you were certain turned back the clock? You can find the following substances in countless skin products from department stores, health food stores or your corner grocery store. You may be surprised at what cannot help your skin.

Collagen and Elastin

Collagen and elastin add to the structural integrity of the skin. Loss of these leads to wrinkles and facial sagging. Replenishing collagen and elastin in the dermis may reverse signs of aging. If collagen is so great, why not put it directly on the skin? Because these large proteins cannot penetrate skin deeply enough to have a lasting effect, making creams with collagen and elastin useless.

On the positive side, collagen injections can plump up skin, filling in wrinkles for three to four months. If you have injections every two to three months, you will need less collagen each time and ultimately save money.

Placenta Extract

Some cosmetic companies claim that placenta extract increases blood flow to the skin and aids in cell growth and function. However, no scientific evidence substantiates these claims.

Amniotic Fluid

Amniotic fluid has been added to topical preparations in hopes that it could penetrate the skin and promote cell growth. This theory has not been proven.

Hormone Creams

Researchers are still questioning whether a topically applied cream can maintain healthy collagen or promote the production of new collagen. There are a few studies involving an estrogen cream that show it might be beneficial.

Save Your Money, Save Your Face

When it comes to cosmetics, most just act as high priced moisturizers. If they don't have proven ingredients, pass them up. Over the years, patients have constantly asked, "What products will really work for my particular skin?" My research has shown me what active ingredients actually improve the health and appearance of a person's skin. But my patients have had a hard time finding products with these ingredients. Therefore, I provided a line of cleansers, nutrients, moisturizers and sunscreens, so I could make certain that my patients had access to the right ingredients, with the right pH and combination for their skin. In the tear out pages at the end of this book, I recommend the right products for different skin types. I also include the specific product from my private line that fits the bill. This way you have the choice to research cosmetics on your own, knowing what to look for, or to try this private line already designed within these guidelines.

Chapter 6

BEAUTY STARTS IN THE BATHROOM

Your Daily Skin Care Routine

Traditionally, washing your face involves good old soap and water. Though many have heard the warning, most people still lather up washcloths, rub their faces, then rinse the washcloths off and wipe their faces clean. **If you wash your face this way, STOP IT NOW!**

A better way to wash your face

1. A washcloth scratches and tugs your skin, while scrubbing essential oils away. Instead begin by using your hands to rinse your face with water.

2. Gently rub cleanser on your face with your hands.

3. Rinse your face thoroughly by splashing lukewarm water on it.

4. Gently pat your face dry with a towel or soft cloth. Brushes, louffahs and other skin buffers are even rougher than washcloths. Unless recommended by your dermatologist, don't use them on your face.

The Truth About Soap

When caring for your skin, select products that contain ingredients that work. This will make all the difference.

Skin Cleansers

Soaps and detergents remove dirt, body oils and bacteria, while preventing odor and infection. Washing strips your skin of organic fat (lipids), which you need to maintain skin's moisture. Soap can dry your skin, causing flaking, itching and irritation.

Generally, soaps have too high a pH for your skin. Skin is slightly acidic with a pH of 5 or 6. Most soaps have a pH around 10. Even if you have oily skin, you do not want to strip your skin of all its natural oils.

Unfortunately, soap companies do not include the pH balance of their products on their wrappers. Here is an overview of soaps and cleansers:

1. If you generally find soaps too drying, I recommend a **water-soluble cleanser**. You might want to experiment with several to find the one that feels best to you.

2. **Beauty bars or cleansers** are often created to match your skin's pH more closely. They may also have added moisturizers. In liquid form they can be even less drying to your skin.

3. **Transparent soaps** (ones you can see through) usually have a low pH, as well as more natural fats. They don't strip your skin as much as other soaps. But they may clog your pores if you have acne.

4. **Natural soaps** are usually harsher than synthetic ones because they are not specially made to match your skin's acidity. "Natural" does not mean better in this case.

5. **Castile soaps** contain olive oil, but are not any milder than other gentle soaps. Other ingredients can make them irritating.

6. **Antibacterial, deodorant, and acne soaps** are too harsh for most people's faces. They dry out your skin in general and are not recommended. If you use acne soap for extreme breakouts, use it only once a day. If it irritates your skin, try using it every other day.

7. Many women use **cold cream** for removing make-up. You should not depend on these or other heavy, oily cleansing creams to clean your face. You are better off using a mild, water-soluble cleanser for both removing make-up and cleaning your skin.

People with dry skin should choose a mild cleanser, shower with cool water, and apply a moisturizer immediately after bathing.

Moisturizers

Moisturizers prevent your skin from losing water by either layering an oily substance over the skin to keep water in, or by attracting water to the outer skin layer from the inner skin layer. Substances that stop water loss include petrolatum, mineral oil, lanolin, and silicone. Glycerin, propylene glycol, proteins and some vitamins attract water to your face. However, you can become allergic to any of these.

As you develop your skin-care routine, refer back to the skin type you determined at the beginning of the book. The best of all possible worlds is a dry-skinned person living in a humid climate or an oily-skinned person living in a dry climate.

Water is the skin's main source of moisture. Most treatments for dry skin add water or trap water in the skin. Both excessive humidity (above 90%) and low humidity (less than 10 %) break down your outer skin barrier. For the skin to appear and feel normal, the water content of this layer must be above 10 %, ideally between 20 and 35%.

You need to clean your skin without removing all of the natural moisturizers, then put something on to retain moisture.

Immediately after cleansing your face, apply a product containing hyaluronic acid to help nutrients and moisturizers penetrate more deeply into the skin. You're best off applying creams that stimulate collagen formation and thicker skin, like Renova, Tazorac or a glucosamine containing product.

Finally, put on a moisturizer with sunscreen in the daytime and a moisturizer with antioxidants in the evening to complete your routine.

The Toner Myth

Toners, solutions generally high in alcohol, are supposed to clean skin as well as tighten pores. Most people get little benefit from a toner. If you have oily skin, it may temporarily dry your skin out and give you a surface cleansing. However, toners don't clean pores deeply or affect how much oil your skin produces.

Almost all department store cosmetic sales people will try to sell you a toner with their skin care regimen. Politely turn them down. A good cleanser and moisturizer should be everything you need.

1. Toners do not tighten pores.
2. Toners often irritate your skin (that's what the tingly feeling means)
3. You are better off finding a good cleanser to remove dirt, make-up and excess oil than relying on a toner to do it.

Facial Masks

Women and some men have long viewed facials as a beauty luxury. Not only does your aesthetician pamper you, but your skin feels noticeably different afterwards. Facials can increase circulation in the skin, and may remove a thin layer of dead skin cells. The steam portion of the facial causes skin to sweat, which does not truly cleanse your pores, but it can hydrate your skin.

The facial massage during this treatment can feel good and make your skin rosier with the increased blood flow. However, the massage must be gentle, otherwise it can aggravate pimples, break capillaries, and otherwise damage skin.

Scrubbing and exfoliation may prove too harsh for some skin. Request an alpha hydroxy scrub for the gentlest, most effective exfoliation.

Overall, be skeptical of claims of facial masks bringing miraculous results. They can hydrate the skin and allow topical nutrients to reach the important deeper areas of the skin.

SIMPLE WAYS TO HELP YOUR SKIN

A Boost for Your Skin: Sleep on Your Back

This one is simple and does not involve major lifestyle changes. Gravity pulls on your skin during the day. Over time, sleep lines develop from pressing one side of your face against a pillow. Give it a little break when you sleep. Don't sleep on your side or stomach. Make sleeping on your back a nightly habit and reduce the chance of developing an extra crease on that side of your face.

Smoking: Nothing's Sexier Than a Wrinkled-Up 30-year-old

Over the years we have all heard of the damaging effects that smoking can have on our lungs, heart and blood vessels. However, most people do not know what smoking does to their skin. Besides its other harmful effects, smoking causes skin nearly the same extreme problems that sunlight does. Scientists have found that smokers are almost five times more likely to have wrinkles than nonsmokers.

Smoking leads to the production of a large quantity of free radicals in your skin, damaging the supporting structures. A typical "smoker's" face exhibits prominent wrinkles, gauntness, thin grayish color, and areas of orange, purple and red pigmentation.

You can see cigarettes' well-known aging effects even in your mid-to-late 20s. Nicotine in cigarette smoke cuts down on the skin's oxygen supply by reducing blood flow. Smoking also reduces collagen, the substance that keeps your skin tight and smooth.

Smokers tend to have more problems with wound healing after surgery and have more pronounced scarring. Smoking also increases the risk of developing skin cancers, especially squamous-cell carcinomas. If you smoke, STOP! If you don't, DON'T START!

Slow Down the Face Years Clock

Your daily habits make or break your skin. Wash skin gently. Use products proven to keep skin smooth and healthy. Avoid bad habits like scrunching your face with a pillow, smoking and going outside during the day without sunscreen. Do all of these things and your skin will stay beautiful much longer.

Chapter 7

YOUR FACE SAYS "CHIPS AND DIP" LONG BEFORE YOUR THIGHS DO

You cannot prevent all the signs of time on your skin, but you can hold them at bay pretty effectively. As your largest organ, skin needs as many nutrients as any other part of your body. Research proves that eating right keeps skin cells vibrant, elastic, and resistant.

Fast Food Ages You Fast

Most people do not want to make big changes. They think healthy food will taste like cardboard. Food brings us pleasure and happiness. It's our reward and solace. We eat what we know and what we like.

Food is a habit. In our busy lives, we eat what's convenient. This often means prepackaged meals, full of preservatives and toxic fats. Prepackaged foods, frozen meals, microwavable dishes and easy-mix formulas have much less nutrition than meals with fresh ingredients. Pre-made foods fill your stomach, but they leave your body starving for nutrition. Choosing different foods can feel overwhelming. However, with a few basic principles, you may be surprised at how easily you can eat simple, delicious food that gives you gorgeous skin. You have many reasons to look closer at what you put into your body.

Chemicals Make You Old

Toxic, damaging free radicals attack your skin. They come from both the environment and as a by-product of normal cell functions. Your daily exposure to sun, car fumes, cigarette smoke, cleaning chemicals, and other common free radicals ages you much faster than time. These chemicals damage the structure of your cells. You can slow your skin's aging by getting rid of free radicals and also preventing them from forming in the first place.

Vitamins Make You Beautiful

You need vitamins to look good. The sallow, chapped skin common to people with eating disorders shows what happens when skin does not get the vitamins and nutrients it needs. A high-fat diet saps the immune system that heals your skin. Fat can also lead to changes in your arteries which keeps blood from reaching your skin. A high-fat diet may increase recurrences of skin cancer.

You can help your skin even if you can't avoid pollutants. Antioxidants counteract the danger of free radicals. Your body makes some antioxidants, but not nearly enough for your skin to fight all the free radicals you face in an average day. Boost antioxidants in your skin by eating antioxidants-rich foods, taking vitamins, and applying antioxidant creams to your skin.

You need both water-soluble antioxidants, like vitamin C, and fat-soluble ones, like vitamin E, because skin has watery areas, and a fatty area. All of these need antioxidants to protect them.

Easy Can Be Healthy Too

Skin conditions and inflammations can come from deficiencies of nutrients like vitamin A or essential fatty acids. Though most diets give you these nutrients, even minor deficiencies slow your ability to heal yourself. You need to purposely eat everything your skin and the rest of your body needs.

Changing your diet cannot eliminate all of your wrinkles or stop aging, but what you eat affects every organ, including your skin. Studies show that you can slow or even turn back skin's aging by eating right.

Most of us eat what we're used to, what's easy, and what tastes the best. We may try to eat healthier but often fall back into old habits and urgent cravings.

Even Sun Worshippers Look Younger with Healthy Food

In a recent study, researchers compared the diet, sun exposure, and skin appearance of people in Melbourne, Australia, rural Greece and Sweden. The study proved rumors right. A healthier diet actually made people's skin look less wrinkled, even long time sun worshippers. The diet that helped people's skin the most in this study had more vegetables, olive oil, fish, and legumes, as well as less butter, margarine, full fat milk products, and sugar products.

Free radicals from UV sunlight and unhealthy fats severely harm skin. They damage lipids, proteins, and DNA. Eating a lot of saturated fat damaged skin in study subjects. Eating vegetables, olive oil, and legumes lessened some sun damage. Monounsaturated fatty acids like those found in canola and olive oil protected skin against sun exposure. Taking vitamin C and minerals like calcium, phosphorus, magnesium, iron, and zinc also protected people's skin from UV damage.

Good fats like olive oil can also help your body absorb fat-soluble vitamins and nutrients like vitamin E, lycopene, and isoflavones. The nutrition in these healthy foods and vitamins gives your skin free radical- fighting antioxidants and building blocks that protect and repair it.

You can lessen the sun's aging by eating well and taking vitamins. Unfortunately, even if you avoid the sun, eating fatty meat, other bad fats, or sugar will still make your skin look older. Eating well cannot make up for all of the sun exposure of your lifetime, but it can help your skin. To have the best skin possible, avoid direct sunlight, eat healthy, and take vitamins.

Oil Makes or Breaks Your Skin

Oil is a mixture of saturated, polyunsaturated, and mono-unsaturated fats. Oils affect aging because they can influence inflammation. A diet that minimizes inflammation will reduce aging in your skin.

Our body requires two essential fatty acids—omega-3 (linolenic acid) and omega-6 (linoleic acid). We need them to build and maintain a healthy body. We need to eat these in our food because our bodies cannot make them.

In your body essential fatty acids produce different compounds that affect your skin called prostaglandins. You need the right balance of omega-3 to omega-6 oils. These two essential fatty acids compete because they use the same enzyme to change into different kinds of prostaglandins. Too much of one essential fatty acid keeps your body from using the other. If the ratio of omega-3 to omega-6 is out of balance, your body over-produces certain prostaglandins, while neglecting others. To achieve a healthy balance, you need to eat four parts omega-6 to every one part omega-3. But most people who eat processed western foods eat 20 omega-6 to every one omega-3. Their bodies are way out of balance.

You can easily get enough omega-6 fatty acid, especially from processed foods, hydrogenated vegetable oils, corn oil, safflower oil, sunflower, and peanut oils. With a typical American diet, you won't have a problem getting your daily supply of omega-6. However, eating omega-3s takes effort. The best sources are cold water fish like salmon, mackerel, tuna, sea bass, cod, and sardines, or plants including canola (rapeseed), flaxseed (linseed), soybean oil, walnuts, and pumpkin.

In the ideal 4:1 ratio of omega-6 to omega-3, much of linoleic acid (omega-6) is converted to substances that give you smooth skin, faster healing, and increased blood flow to your skin. They also reduce inflammation, and help you hold water in your skin. However, too much omega-6 creates excessive inflammatory products. If you eat too much omega-6, you reduce how much omega-3 acid your body can produce by as much as 40 percent.

So not only is it hard to get enough omega-3 fatty acids, but eating too much processed foods, butter, or omega-6 cooking oils blocks your levels of the omega-3s in your body.

Inflammation from an excessive amount of Omega-6 makes your skin look old and damaged. To lower your omega-6 intake, use olive or canola oil. Canola and Olive oils contain high levels of monounsaturated fatty acids and don't create harmful inflammation, or raise insulin and cholesterol.

Unprocessed olive oil contains polyphenols, vitamin E and other natural antioxidants that protect you from harmful free radicals. Extra virgin olive oils have undergone the least processing and contain the most healthy ingredients. The deep green color of olive oil comes from the polyphenols, antioxidants that prevent free radicals.

One commonly used fat called trans-fats is extremely harmful to your body. Trans-fats are created when food manufacturers add hydrogen to liquid oils to make them solid at room temperature. Processed foods are notoriously high in unhealthy trans-fatty acids. Regularly eating trans-fatty acids (found in margarine, vegetable shortening, and commercially processed vegetable oils, often referred to as hydrogenated or partially hydrogenated oils) greatly raises your risk for coronary heart disease. Trans-fats can harm you even more than saturated fat.

Read labels on the foods you choose and try to limit foods containing any unhealthy oil or oil that is solid at room temperature. To emphasize how harmful they actually can be, a recent decision by the FDA will require labels on products listing the quantity of trans fat in the product.

Why Sugar Makes You Old
Sugar is the stable of modern food and is in almost every packaged food we eat. The truth is that when sugar combines with protein in our bodies, it forms harmful advanced glycosylation end products (AGEs). These AGEs hurt enzyme systems and keep cells from repairing themselves. AGEs also inflame your skin. In a nutshell, AGEs make you age.

Blood sugar comes from foods high in carbohydrates. After your stomach digests food, glucose enters your bloodstream. Your body responds to more glucose by secreting insulin. Insulin helps the glucose enter liver, muscle, and fat cells. Insulin also stops your body from burning fat and protein for energy. It promotes fat storage and increases fatty substances called triglyerides, which circulate in your blood. HDL, the good cholesterol, falls. LDL, the bad cholesterol, rises.

High insulin levels can lead to the production of arachidonic acid (inflammatory compounds) in the metabolic pathway of omega-6 fatty acids. Higher levels of insulin can also lower vitamin E, an important antioxidant.

What You get From Food

You need excellent nutrition to have beautiful, healthy skin as you age. Most of know that we should eat a healthy diet, but we are unsure or even unaware of what is really healthy for us.

Your skin requires daily levels of protein, carbohydrates, fats, vitamins, phytochemicals, and minerals.

For lovely skin you need vitamins A, C and E, and the right ratio of omega-3 to omega-6 fatty acids. Healthy food keeps skin looking beautiful by preventing inflammation, wrinkles, and other skin conditions. Eat all of the following to have healthy skin.

Protein

Proteins are made up of smaller amino acids. You can only get certain proteins through your diet, but your body can make others. You need protein for tissue growth and to replace and maintain cells. You also need proteins to make enzymes and antibodies. When you are starving, your body uses protein for energy.

Carbohydrates

Carbohydrates give you most of your energy. They mainly come from plants. Simple carbohydrates digest quickly, turning into sugar that enters your blood and raises insulin. Complex carbohydrates, chains of simple sugars bound together, take longer to digest.

Fats

Fats provide energy, act as building blocks for essential chemicals, and carry fat soluble vitamins. Most dietary fat is from a group of chemical compounds.

As was noted earlier, avoid fats that are solid at room temperature. Try to use only olive oil and canola oil in cooking. Be sure to cook oil at lower temperatures for longer, rather than at high temperatures to keep damaging chemicals from forming.

Minerals

Minerals are inorganic elementary substances found in soil and water. The minerals your body needs the most are calcium, phosphorus magnesium, sodium, potassium, and chloride. The others are only needed in small amounts. You need minerals for almost all of your body processes.

Vitamins

You need vitamins in small amounts to have a normal metabolism. Since your body can only make vitamins D, K and the B vitamin biotin, most vitamins have to come from your diet or from supplements. Vitamins are either fat-soluble or water soluble.

Fat-soluble vitamins (A, D, and E) are stored in the body so taking too much of these can be toxic. Your body does not store water-soluble vitamins. You have to keep taking them to have them in your body.

Phytochemicals

Phytochemicals are non-nutritive plant chemicals that contain protective, disease-preventing compounds. Polyphenols are powerful antioxidants. One type of polyphenol is a group called Flavanoids or bioflavanoids which are found in green tea, most fruits and vegetables, as well as nuts, seeds, grains, and soy products. They are also in coffee and red wine.

SOURCES OF PHYTOCHEMICALS				
FLAVANOIDS	CAROTENOIDS	ISOFLAVONES	LYCOPENES	PHENOLIC COMPOUNDS
Citrus Fruits	Carrots	Soy Products	Tomatoes	Red wine
Tomatoes	Sweet	Whole grains	Peppers	Citrus Fruits
Berries	Potatoes	Chick Peas		Tomatoes
Carrots	Nectarines			Peppers
Pumpkins				
Peppers				

Most medical literature lists vitamins A, C and E, and omega-3 fatty acids as necessary for healthy skin

Food Sources Of Vital Vitamins and Fats

The following list identifies foods that are good sources for the top skin nutrients, vitamin A, vitamin C, vitamin E, omega 3, and omega 6.

SOURCES OF VITAL VITAMINS AND FATS				
VITAMIN A	VITAMIN C	VITAMIN E	OMEGA-3	OMEGA-6
Oatmeal	Apply Juice	Almonds	Mackerel	Soybean Oil
(instant fortified)	Cantaloupe	Filberts	Salmon	Peanut Oil
Mango (raw)	Cranberry Juice	Sunflower seeds	Sardines	Sunflower seeds
Carrots	Grapefruit mm	Olive Oil	Anchovies	
Kale	Grape Juice	Flaxseed	Tuna	
Peas & carrots	Honeydew	Canola		
Red pepper	Kiwi	Flaxseed		
Spinach	Mandarin orange	Canola		
Squash	Mango	Soybean		
Sweet potato	Papaya			
Turnip greens	Pineapple			
Turnip	Strawberries			
Beef, calf, pork	Tomatoes			
Chicken/turkey				

Nutritional Supplements

First try to get your nutrients from food. Foods have fiber, water, and other beneficial ingredients besides the specific nutrients in supplements. If you cannot get enough nutrients from food, consider taking the following supplements:

CoEnzyme Q10 helps your cells make energy. This antioxidant also may help regenerate vitamin E.

Fish oil supplements give you a concentrated sources of essential fatty acids. They usually contain two omega-3 fatty acids, Eicosopentaenoic acid (EPA) and docosahexaenoic acid (DHA). To determine how many grams of omega-3 fats are in a capsule, look for the abbreviations EPA and DHA. Take 1 to 2 grams per day. Look for one with no cholesterol, which is purer than regular fish oil products. If capsules taste bad to you, try liquid forms, which have less after taste.

Evening Primrose is a good source of linoleic and gamma linoleic acid. The dose is usually 3 to 8 grams a day.

Borage and black currant oils are much richer in gamma linoleic acid. 2 to 3 grams a day is the correct dose.

Top Ten Foods to Avoid

A list of foods that harm your skin would take up a book in itself, so I narrowed it down to the top ten foods to avoid to have beautiful, healthy skin. Changing your diet requires discipline and an open mind, but I will try to make it easier for you. You can first cut down on the unhealthy foods you eat the most. The foods I warn against harm your skin in different ways. Some have saturated fats, others cause sudden and wide swings in sugar levels, skyrocketing your insulin, while others have harmful levels of fatty acids. You absolutely need protein for good health, but protein high in saturated fat and omega-6 fatty acids may do more harm than good. Ground beef, sausage, and bacon have a very high fat to protein ratio: Exactly the opposite of how you should choose protein for your diet. They are also cooked at high temperatures, creating even more harm to your skin. Saturated fats are known to hurt your heart and blood system but recent studies also show that saturated fat increases skin's aging and wrinkling. As I've discussed, trans fatty acids have extremely harmful effects regarding skin health and appearance.

Carbohydrates include foods that you might not think of as carbs. Ones that cause sudden and high levels of blood glucose levels, e.g. raisins, pasta, or baked beans, inflame and damage our skin. While legumes have positive benefits, baked beans commercially prepared with brown sugar or molasses spike your blood sugar. Also, cooking beans at high heat or for a long time causes cell walls to break down which allows the sugar content to be rapidly absorbed.

FOODS TO AVOID						
PROTEINS	FATS	CARBOHYDRATES				
		VEGETABLES	FRUITS	DAIRY	BEANS & LEGUMES	WHOLE GRAINS
Ground Beef Sausage Bacon	Trans fatty acids (Partially Hydrogenated Vegetable oils) Butter	French Fries	Raisins	Full fat Ice Cream	Baked Beans	Pasta

If I had to pick the #1 food to avoid, I would pick one of America's favorites, the French fry. It has it all: A carbohydrate that causes a rapid rise in blood sugar, and is fried at high temperature in trans fatty acids. Cooking a carbohydrate at such a high temperature creates acrylamide, a substance believed to cause cancer. Don't forget to avoid the French fry's close relative, the potato chip. It isn't any better.

Your Food Is Written All Over Your Face

Though many people think a balanced diet including fruits and vegetables will supply their bodies' needs, our modern diet of preserved, transported and manufactured foods has fewer vitamins than it used to have. Prior to the 1950s people ate locally grown fruits and vegetables shortly after picking them. This allowed them to ripen and absorb the most vitamins possible. Today shippers transport produce across the country or from other countries. Picked less ripe, this produce doesn't absorb as many nutrients. In addition, the vitamins in fruits and vegetables start to decay as soon as they are removed from the plant.

All methods of food preservation destroy vitamins. Modern fruits and vegetables have about 20-30% fewer vitamins than produce consumed in the 50s. Moreover, less than half the population eats even one serving of fruits or vegetables a day. Even if you eat a very healthy diet, you may not get the level of nutrition you need through food alone.

In this fast-paced, fast-food-oriented society, a diet rich in fruits and vegetable, and eating fish two to three times a week can help your skin look younger and smoother.

Foods rich in antioxidants, green leafy vegetables, beans, olive oil, nuts and multigrain breads may fend off environmental damage to skin. Eating foods with high levels of antioxidants such as Vitamins A, C and E can give you smoother skin.

Our bodies and skin also require essential fatty acids for normal growth and development. You need omega-6 to give your body the inflammatory abilities that fight infection. You need enough omega-3 fatty acids to prevent too much inflammation and resulting skin damage. Since our bodies don't make these essential omega-3 and omega-6 fatty acids, they must be supplied in our diets. Our goal should be to consume four parts omega-6 to one part omega-3.

Vitamins: A Turbo Charge for Your Skin

Our skin's health depends on beta carotene, vitamin A, vitamin C and vitamin E. These antioxidants protect skin from sun damage. Vitamin A helps keep skin elastic and smooth. Extreme vitamin B complex deprivation can even lead to a rare condition that causes flaky eczema. Vitamin C is a potent antioxidant and also aids in collagen formation.

Antioxidants control the premature aging process by interfering with the first step of the pathway, the generation of free radicals. Although our skin contains many antioxidants, excessive ultraviolet light exposure can deplete the antioxidants in our skin, causing us to age faster. We also encounter free radicals every day, through cigarette smoke, car exhaust, radiation, pollution, chemicals in our water and air, and alcohol. Believe it or not, we continuously produce free radicals in our body as we convert food to energy and as a natural function of respiration and metabolism.

Free radicals damage capillary and nerve endings as well as elastin and collagen, leading to aging and wrinkles. Antioxidants are our allies in this constant war on our skin. They help neutralize the havoc that free radicals wreak on our bodies. This process destroys the antioxidants but protects your cells. You can always take more antioxidants.

Another Lecture on Working Out (But a Really Short One)

You already know that exercise makes you look and feel better. It helps skin by increasing circulation, releasing toxins and increasing muscle mass, which keeps skin anchored and prevents sagging. Aerobic activity burns fat that threatens overall health, including the immune system, which keeps skin rejuvenating itself.

I promised it would be short.

Chapter 8

HOW TO CHECK YOUR HEALTH: LOOK AT YOUR FACE

SKIN CONDITIONS

Acne

The scourge of teens everywhere, excessive breakouts of acne cause stress, embarrassment and life-long scars. For most people acne clears up after adolescence, and many have no noticeable scars. Still, it can be successfully treated with prescription medication.

Acne Myths

MYTH #1   Acne is caused by poor hygiene, not by dirt or surface skin oils.

Washing may help in the overall treatment of acne by removing excess oils, dead skin cells and foreign substances, but washing alone will not clear it up or prevent it. The best approach to hygiene and acne: Wash your face twice a day with a mild soap, pat dry, and use a prescription acne treatment.

MYTH #2   Acne is caused by diet.

Extensive scientific studies have not found a conclusive connection between diet and acne. In other words, food does not cause acne. Not chocolate. Not French fries. Not pizza. Nonetheless, some people insist that certain foods affect their acne. If that is the case, avoid those foods. However, as was pointed out in the previous chapters, eating a balanced, nutritious diet can have a dramatic effect on the health and the degree of inflammation that occurs in your skin. Acne is an inflammatory disease so although we cannot specifically implicate chocolate or pizza as the cause, a healthy diet together with proper medical treatment, will bring about the best control of acne.

MYTH #3   Acne is simply a cosmetic disease.

It does affect the way people look and does not otherwise pose a threat to your health. However, acne can result in permanent scars. Acne itself, as well as its scars, can affect the way people feel about themselves and touch their whole lives.

MYTH #4   You have to let acne just run its course.

The truth is, acne can be treated successfully. If the acne products you have tried haven't worked, there are many different medications available to control the problem. With the products available today, there is no reason why anyone has to endure acne or get acne scars.

So What Works for Acne?

You need to deal with two basic conditions when treating acne. First, you need an individualized program to prevent or minimize the major cause of acne – plugged oil-gland openings. Many medications effectively control this problem – e.g. Retin-A, Azelex, Differin, or Tazorac.

Second, you need to prevent the overgrowth of bacteria in the plugged oil glands. You can do this with antibacterial lotions, gels, creams or oral antibiotics.

In severe cases the use of a medication, Accutane, may be prescribed. This medication is a vitamin A derivative and works very well. However, it needs to be monitored closely because of occasional side effects. Pregnancy must be avoided while on the medication. Periodic blood tests and regular appointments are necessary during the 16-to-20 week treatment.

Depending on your skin type, the type of acne, and the number of inflamed lesions, different medications or combination of these medications can be prescribed. These medications will minimize the severity of acne and help prevent permanent marks or scarring.

Acne Rosacea

Acne rosacea is a common form of adult acne that occurs most often in fair-skinned Celtic or Scandinavian people over 30 years old. The condition often begins with redness in the center of the face. The redness gradually becomes more persistent. "Broken" or dilated blood vessels known as telangiectasia appear, as well as small, red acne-like papules and pustules.

Unfortunately, no one knows exactly what causes rosacea. Try to avoid the triggers that flush your skin. The most common food triggers include alcohol, spicy foods, hot beverages, cheese, vanilla and chocolate.

Oral or topical antibiotics usually help the inflammation (the papules and pustules). The most commonly used antibiotics are the tetracycline class (tetracycline, doxycycline, or minocycline). Creams with metronidazole or sulfa-based antibiotics can work wonders. If the redness persists, lasers or pulsed light can remove the blood vessels.

Eczema

The term eczema refers to a number of conditions related to inflamed skin. You might inherit it or get it from excessive dryness or exposure to an irritant. Moisturizers and topical steroids usually control the problem fairly quickly. Low-potency hydrocortisone is available as an over-the-counter medication. Stronger topical steroids must be prescribed by a physician.

Dandruff

Dandruff is often associated with a mild inflammation of the scalp's skin. The inflammation leads to a more rapid cell turnover causing dry, shedding skin.

Anti-dandruff shampoos often contain tar or salicylic acid. If these do not work, a prescription topical steroid helps and won't hurt you.

Precancerous Lesions

Actinic keratoses are precancerous lesions that can progress and develop into skin cancer. They are easily treated by light freezing with liquid nitrogen. They appear as dry, scaly scabs or red patches that don't heal.

Skin Cancer

There are three main types of skin cancer in order of frequency: Basal cell carcinoma (800,000 new cases each year), squamous cell carcinoma (200,000 new cases each year), and malignant melanoma (51,000 new cases each year). The first two usually appear as a slowly growing, non-healing sore. Melanomas are most often pigmented lesions with irregular borders and irregular pigmentation. All of these need prompt attention by a physician.

Did You Know?

- Your skin is your body's largest organ.

- If your skin were removed, it would weigh between seven and nine pounds and stretch out to about 20 square feet.

- One square inch of skin is packed with 100 oil glands, 15 feet of blood vessels and two kinds of sweat glands.

- It takes about an ounce of sunscreen to protect all of your exposed skin from the sun. An ounce of sunscreen is enough to fill up a shot glass.

- Smoking robs your skin of life-giving oxygen. Nicotine narrows blood vessels and prevents oxygen-carrying blood from circulating through the tiny capillaries in the top layers of the skin.

- You should apply your sunscreen at least 20 minutes before going into the sun so it has time to absorb into your skin.

- Skin has a memory. It keeps track of all of the sun damage that's accumulated over the years. Even normal, everyday sun exposure can cause lines and wrinkles.

Chapter 9

"WHO'S HER DOCTOR?" SEARCHING FOR "DR. RIGHT"

The doctor you choose may make a bigger difference than the products and procedures you select. The insurance industry has made it difficult for many doctors to make a living wage practicing healing medicine. As a result, more doctors have taken up elective procedures because patients pay for these themselves. Doctors from very diverse fields have entered the field. Their training and back- ground vary widely. Patients must take the initiative to find out about their doctors.

Your Doctor Makes the Difference

If you take a piece of stone and give it to a carpenter or give it to Michelangelo, the results will be dramatically different. With any procedure, fine but important technical points can make huge differences in the final outcome. Unfortunately, there is no Board Certification for physicians regarding laser procedures as there is for medical specialties like dermatology and internal medicine. You must screen your own doctor for experience and skill.

Follow These Steps to Choose a Doctor

1. Decide what you will have done.

2. Find out about the doctor's experience with the procedure. How long has he or she performed it? On how many patients? There is no substitute for experience.

   a. Experience also includes attending seminars and educational meetings.

b. In addition to seminars, before I begin performing a procedure I spend time with one of the first or most experienced physician with that procedure. Find out all the experience your potential doctor has with the procedure.

3. Ask to see photos of patients. Physicians should encourage you to speak to some of their patients.

4. Ask to speak to their patients.

5. Ask about complications they have.

6. Ask what type of physician they are: General practice, allergist, plastic surgeon, etc. If they normally have not been trained to do this procedure, (allergists, etc.), the decision to perform these procedures may be made solely for monetary reasons. A two-day course in Hawaii doesn't count as "trained."

   a. Dermatologists are trained to have a deep understanding of skin, extremely important for the procedure, but even more essential during the healing phase. If problems or potential problems occur, a dermatologist has expertise for all types of skin problems.

   b. You want a specialist in your area. I have heard of allergists, pediatricians, and even oral surgeons doing laser resurfacing.

   Remember, it is your skin on the line, so don't be afraid to ask questions and insist on the best. Don't let doctors intimidate you or gloss over their experience. You have a right to demand the best care.

Chapter 10

LOOKING BEAUTIFUL JUST GOT A WHOLE LOT EASIER

Quick Reference Guide

FACE YEARS:	**Treatments:**
20 - 25	Skin care regimen

Tretinoin (Renova or Retin-A) or Tazarotene (Tazorac)
Salt peels or acid peels weekly, bimonthly or monthly, depending on skin damage

Botox for furrows in brow or forehead

Wear sunscreen EVERYDAY

(Apply a shot-glass full for whole body coverage.)

Check sunscreen for:
At least 30 SPF

BOTH UVA and UVB protection

Look for Parasol 1789, effective against UVA rays

Vitamins C and E for added sun protection

Waterproof sunscreen that lasts for 5-6 hours instead of one hour

Sunscreen for your skin type: Oily skin needs gel products and dry skin types should use lotion products.

FACE YEARS:	**Treatments:**
26 - 34	Skin care regimen

Tretinoin (Renova or Retin-A) or Tazarotene (Tazorac)

Salt peels or acid peels weekly, bimonthly or monthly, depending on skin damage

Botox for furrows in brow or forehead

Salt peels

Light chemical peels

Non-ablative lasers

Perhaps collagen-filling injections

Wear sunscreen EVERYDAY

(Apply a shot-glass full for whole body coverage.)

Check sunscreen for:
At least 30 SPF

BOTH UVA and UVB protection

Look for Parasol 1789, effective against UVA rays

Vitamins C and E for added sun protection

Waterproof sunscreen that lasts for 5-6 hours instead of one hour

Sunscreen for your skin type: Oily skin needs gel products and dry skin types should use lotion products.

FACE YEARS: **Treatments:**
35 - 49 Skin care regimen

Tretinoin (Renova or Retin-A) or Tazarotene (Tazorac)

Salt peels or acid peels weekly, bimonthly or monthly, depending on skin damage

Botox for furrows in brow, forehead

Deeper chemical peels (Tricholoroacetic Acid)

Laser resurfacing mostly around mouth and eyes

Non-ablative lasers

Pulsed-light Treatments

Radio-Frequency Skin Tightening

Laser blepharoplasty for droopy eyelids or fat protrusion of lower eyelids.

Wear sunscreen EVERYDAY

(Apply a shot-glass full for whole body coverage.)

Check sunscreen for:

At least 30 SPF

BOTH UVA and UVB protection

Look for Parasol 1789, effective against UVA rays

Vitamins C and E for added sun protection

Waterproof sunscreen that lasts for 5-6 hours instead of one hour

Sunscreen for your skin type: Oily skin needs gel products and dry skin types should use lotion products.

FACE YEARS:	**Treatments:**
50 - 64	Skin care regimen

Tretinoin (Renova or Retin-A) or Tazarotene (Tazorac)

Salt Peels or acid peels weekly, bimonthly or monthly, depending on skin sensitivity

Botox for furrows in brow, forehead

Laser rejuvenation would involve full face

Non-ablative lasers

Pulsed-light Treatments

Radio-Frequency Skin Tightening

Laser blepharoplasty for droopy eyelids or fat protrusion of lower eyelids

Wear sunscreen EVERYDAY

(Apply a shot-glass full for whole body coverage.)

Check sunscreen for:

At least 30 SPF

BOTH UVA and UVB protection

Look for Parasol 1789, effective against UVA rays

Vitamins C and E for added sun protection

Waterproof sunscreen that lasts for 5-6 hours instead of one hour

Sunscreen for your skin type: Oily skin needs gel products and dry skin types should use lotion products.

FACE YEARS:	**Treatments:**
65 - 75	Skin care regimen

Tretinoin (Renova or Retin-A) or Tazarotene (Tazorac)

Salt peels or acid peels weekly, bimonthly or monthly, depending on skin damage

Botox for furrows in brow, forehead

Laser rejuvenation would involve full face

Non-Ablative Lasers

Pulsed-light Treatments

Radio-Frequency Skin Tightening

Laser blepharoplasty for droopy eyelids or fat protrusion of lower eyelids

Wear sunscreen EVERYDAY

(Apply a shot-glass full for whole body coverage.)

Check sunscreen for:

At least 30 SPF

BOTH UVA and UVB protection

Look for Parasol 1789, effective against UVA rays

Vitamins C and E for added sun protection

Waterproof sunscreen that lasts for 5-6 hours instead of one hour

Sunscreen for your skin type: Oily skin needs gel products and dry skin types should use lotion products.

The following are the skin care regimens that I recommend for my patients depending on their skin type. The products listed are those which I have developed in order to provide ingredients which I feel are essential to topical skin nutrition and repair. These products are available online or by contacting my office. If you decide to use your own products, you should check to be certain that they contain the important ingredients that follow.

NORMAL SKIN **Morning**

Cleanse with **AHA Facial Cleanser:** Alpha Hydroxy Acids

Apply **Hydrating B Serum:** Sodium Hyaluronate, Marine Enzyme (MDI Complex), Beta-Glucan

Apply **C-Collagen Gel:** Glusoamine HCL, Ergothioneine, Vitamin C, Marine Enzyme (MDI complex)

Apply **Eye Repair Cream:** Acetyl Hexapeptide-3, Hyaluronic acid, Martixyl, Marine Enzyme (MDI Complex), Beta-glucan.

Apply **Solar Protection System SPF 30:** Octinoxate, Octisalate, Oxybenzone,Avobenzone (Parsol 1789).

Apply **Tri-Lipid Enhancer:** Ceramide, Sphingolipids, Cholesterol) Vitamin C, Vitamin E.

Evening

Cleanse with **AHA Facial Cleanser:** Alpha Hydroxy Acids

Apply **Hydrating B Serum:** Sodium Hyaluronate, Marine Enzyme (MDI Complex), Beta-Glucan

Apply **C-Collagen Gel:**Glusoamine HCL, Ergothioneine, Vitamin C, Marine Enzyme (MDI complex)

Apply **Eye Repair Cream:** Acetyl Hexapeptide-3, Hyaluronic acid, Martixyl, Marine Enzyme (MDI Complex), Beta-glucan.

Apply Tretinoin (Renova or Retin-A) or Tazarotene (Tazorac): Requires prescription

Apply **Night Repair Cream:** Ubiquinone, Hyaluronic Acid, Matrixyl, Marine Enzyme (MDI complex),Beta-glucan, Niacinamide

Apply **Tri-Lipid Enhancer:** Ceramide, Sphingolipids, Cholesterol) Vitamin C, Vitamin E.

SENSITIVE SKIN **Morning**

Cleanse with **Enzyme Facial Cleanser:** Mild desquamating cleanser

Apply **Hydrating B Serum:** Sodium Hyaluronate, Marine Enzyme (MDI Complex), Beta-Glucan

Apply **C-Collagen Gel:** Glusoamine HCL, Ergothioneine, Vitamin C, Marine Enzyme (MDI complex)

Apply **Eye Repair Cream:** Acetyl Hexapeptide-3, Hyaluronic acid, Martixyl, Marine Enzyme (MDI Complex), Beta-glucan.

Apply **Solar Protection System SPF 30:** Octinoxate, Octisalate, Oxybenzone,Avobenzone (Parsol 1789). Vitamin C, Vitamin E.

Apply **Tri-Lipid Enhancer:** Ceramide, Sphingolipids, Cholesterol) Vitamin C, Vitamin E.

Evening

Cleanse with **Enzyme Facial Cleanser:** Mild desquamating cleanser

Apply **Hydrating B Serum:** Sodium Hyaluronate, Marine Enzyme (MDI Complex), Beta-Glucan

Apply **C-Collagen Gel:** Glusoamine HCL, Ergothioneine, Vitamin C, Marine Enzyme (MDI complex)

Apply **Eye Repair Cream:** Acetyl Hexapeptide-3, Hyaluronic acid, Martixyl, Marine Enzyme (MDI Complex), Beta-glucan.

Apply **Night Repair Cream:** Ubiquinone, Hyaluronic Acid, Matrixyl, Marine Enzyme (MDI complex),Beta-glucan, Niacinamide

Apply **Tri-Lipid Enhancer:** Ceramide, Sphingolipids, Cholesterol) Vitamin C, Vitamin E.

OILY SKIN **Morning**

Cleanse with **AHA Facial Cleanser:** Alpha Hydroxy Acids

Apply **Hydrating B Serum:** Sodium Hyaluronate, Marine Enzyme (MDI Complex), Beta-Glucan

Apply **C-Collagen Gel:**Glusoamine HCL, Ergothioneine, Vitamin C, Marine Enzyme (MDI complex)

Apply **Eye Repair Cream:** Acetyl Hexapeptide-3, Hyaluronic acid, Martixyl, Marine Enzyme (MDI Complex), Beta-glucan.

Apply **Solar Protection System Oil Free SPF 30:** Zinc Oxide, Octyl Methoxycinnamate active ingredients.

Evening

Cleanse with **AHA Facial Cleanser:** Alpha Hydroxy Acids

Apply **Hydrating B Serum:** Sodium Hyaluronate, Marine Enzyme (MDI Complex), Beta-Glucan

Apply **C-Collagen Gel:** Glusoamine HCL, Ergothioneine, Vitamin C, Marine Enzyme (MDI complex)

Apply **Eye Repair Cream:** Acetyl Hexapeptide-3, Hyaluronic acid, Martixyl, Marine Enzyme (MDI Complex), Beta-glucan.

Apply Tretinoin (Renova or Retin-A) or Tazarotene (Tazorac): Requires prescription

Apply **Antioxidant Facial Cream:** Ubiquinone, Marine Enzyme (MDI Complex), Matrixyl, Hyaluronic acid, Niacinamide.

Self Improvement Options

Plump Up	Moisturizer Hyaluronic acid
Cover Up	Make-Up
Protect	Sunscreen
Prevent	Sunscreen
Exfoliate	AHAs Salt Peels Aluminum Oxide Peels
Topical Medications	Tretinoin(Renova or Retin-A) or Tazarotene (Tazorac) Vitamin C Vitamin E. KTTKS Niacinamide Beta-glucan MDI
Rejuvenation	Trichloroacetic Acid or Phenol Peels
Fill In	Collagen Fat Ultra Soft Form Implants
Muscle Relaxant for Expression Lines	Botox

Lasers, Pulsed Light, Radio-frequency

Brown Spots   Nd:YAG, Pulsed-light

Facial Blood Vessels   Nd:YAG, V-Star, V Beam,
                           Pulsed-light

Rejuvenation   Carbon Dioxide, Erbium,
                           Non ablative Radio Frequency

Eyelid Surgery   Carbon Dioxide

Hair Removal   LightSheer Laser,
                           Pulsed-light

Cosmetic Surgery   Face Lift
Brow Lift

Contact Us

If you have any further questions or would like more information, please contact:

http://www.asarchcenter.com
Email: drasarch@asarchcenter.com

Asarch Center for Dermatology and Laser
3701 South Clarkson Street
4th Floor
Englewood, CO 80113

Phone 303.761.7797

Richard G. Asarch, M.D.

Dr. Asarch is a native of Des Moines, Iowa. He received his undergraduate Bachelor of Science Degree from the University of Iowa, and is a graduate of the University of Iowa College of Medicine. Dr. Asarch completed his internship at Good Samaritan Hospital in Portland, Oregon. He served as a General Medical Officer in the United States Air Force before accepting a research fellowship in the Department of Otolaryngology and Maxillofacial Surgery at the University of Iowa where he also completed a year of General Surgery Residency. His Dermatology Residency was completed at the University of Colorado Health Sciences Center, which allowed him the opportunity to study with Dr. Frederic Mohs in Madison Wisconsin to learn the Mohs Micrographic Surgery procedure.

In 1981, four years after entering private practice in his native Iowa, Dr. Asarch was recruited to create and head the Dermatologic Surgery Program and Mohs Micrographic Surgery section for the Department of Dermatology at the University of Colorado Health Sciences Center where he is currently an Associate Clinical Professor of Dermatology. Since 1982, he has run a private practice emphasizing surgical and laser procedures of the skin. In 1999 and in 2003, Dr. Asarch was selected as one of the top dermatologists in the United States by Top Doctors in America.

Maria West

Author Maria West has a background in writing, education and marketing. A graduate of Mills College in Oakland, California, her previous work includes the recently published *Is Half the World Crazy?* And the upcoming *Hell is Hell No Matter How Often You Remodel.* She resides in San Diego, California with her partner, Allen Fahden.